GOD'S
WAITING ROOM

RICK YOHN

A M
P.O. BOX 6000,   934

D1509067

The Navigators is an international Christian
organization. Jesus Christ gave His followers the
Great Commission to go and make disciples
(Matthew 28:19). The aim of The Navigators is
to help fulfill that commission by multiplying
laborers for Christ in every nation.

NavPress is the publishing ministry of The Navigators. NavPress publications are tools to help
Christians grow. Although publications alone
cannot make disciples or change lives, they can
help believers learn biblical discipleship, and
apply what they learn to their lives and
ministries.

Printed in the United States of America

Contents

1
Waiting for God

About two years ago my wife was in a California hospital. Each time I went to visit her, I entered through the emergency entrance, where I passed a large waiting room. Sometimes there were many people in it, at other times only a few. But someone was always there—waiting.

That hospital waiting room seemed to epitomize another experience I was having in my life at that time. I was also waiting. But my waiting room was not in the hospital. It was more a state of being, lasting almost a year. I had just resigned as pastor from my church one month prior to visiting Linda in the hospital. The resignation was to take effect within a few weeks of the visit. I made my decision on the basis that I had taken the church as far as I could under my leadership. A small but militant resistance movement was under way, determined to change the existing leadership. After much prayer, counsel, Scripture reading, and waiting for God to change hearts, I concluded that this chapter of my life was about to close, that the Lord had something new He was about to do.

However, at that point in my life I had no plans for the future. I was emotionally drained and somewhat confused about what God was doing and why He allowed events to go the way they had. With Linda in the hospital recovering from surgery, my job coming to a halt within weeks, and no plans for the future, we entered God's waiting room.

WHAT IS GOD'S WAITING ROOM?

Entering God's waiting room was *no voluntary decision* on my part. I did not want that waiting experience any more than I wanted to wait in the hospital while my wife was having back surgery. I could think of one hundred other things I'd rather do than wait on something to happen over which I had no control.

That was another problem. *I could not determine the outcome.* For so many years I was able to predict, with fair accuracy, what effect my decisions would have on people or circumstances around me. At this time in my life, though, I could not determine what would happen to the church I was leaving, where I would be going for a new ministry, how Linda would recover from surgery, or what people would read into my decision to resign. I was in the position of living one day at a time, completely dependent on the Lord's purpose in these matters.

This waiting period was also characterized as *a place of high stress.* Anyone who has taken a child, wife, or husband to the hospital for emergency treatment has felt the stress level rise significantly as he awaits the doctor's report. God's waiting room is no different. I felt the stress of the circumstances. I felt "beaten down." I wanted out. I searched for answers. I was hoping everything would somehow be like it used to be. But it wasn't, and I was not sure how to handle the outcome.

Also, I faced the issue of *my own inadequacy*. Since I felt so helpless, I had to decide to what degree I could trust God in this situation. Self-sufficiency was no longer a resource from which I could draw wisdom, strength, or control.

Furthermore, I discovered God's waiting room was *a place where God would gradually unfold the next chapter of my life.* He did not give me all the answers at once. In fact, some of my questions may never be answered. But as I waited patiently, I began to see a pattern emerge. What seemed to be mere fragments of isolated events began to form a beautiful mosaic.

Another aspect of God's waiting room I experienced was a great deal of *perplexity*. My waiting generated many questions in my mind. For example: "Why has God brought me to this place?" "What have I done to deserve this?"

Finally, I also had to deal with another issue. Is God's waiting room a place primarily for those who have committed some great sin? A place of punishment? A place where God would get even with me for past mistakes?

WHO ENTERS GOD'S WAITING ROOM?

A wife is patiently waiting for her husband to come to his senses and return to his family after having an affair with a younger woman. She doesn't understand how this could have happened in their marriage. She asks herself, "What did I do wrong? Why would God have allowed this to happen to me?"

Jim, a young business executive, has been riding the road of success for the past several years. Whatever he touched turned to profit. But things are different today. His partners have made some drastic decisions that run contrary to his Christian convictions, and the result could throw the entire business into bankruptcy. His hands are tied. There is nothing he can do to change the situation. He's now awaiting the outcome.

Shirley has been told by the doctor that the lumps on her breast are malignant. He recommends a mastectomy. She dreads the thought of such an ordeal, and is praying that God will intervene and heal her. However, she also realizes that if something isn't done soon, she will no longer have a choice to make. It could then be too late. How long should she wait?

Harry cheerfully drove to work the other morning and noticed that everyone in the office looked so gloomy. He cracked a joke with the intent of cheering up his fellow workers and friends, then walked into his office and sat behind the desk. Within minutes the boss called Harry into his office and hesitantly broke the news: "Harry, you know that money's been tight around here. Our sales are off drastically and the overhead is eating us alive. I'm sorry, Harry. We have to let you go."

These are just a few scenarios taken from real life experiences—the kind of experiences that plunge people into excruciating turmoil. Some individuals never fully recover. Others go through a very difficult period of adjustment with questionable results. As each individual faces a whole new set of circumstances, he enters an uncharted phase of his life. A waiting period.

As I've studied the Scriptures while going through the waiting process, I've discovered that God brings two basic types of people into His special room: those who are spiritually fruitful and those who need further training under God's loving hand of discipline. The remainder of this chapter is devoted to the first of these types: the spiritually fruitful.

DESCRIPTION OF THE SPIRITUALLY FRUITFUL

Who are the spiritually fruitful? Consider the words of the Lord as He spoke to His disciples: "I am the true vine, and my Father is the gardener. He cuts off every branch in me that bears no fruit, while every branch that does bear fruit he prunes so that it will be even more fruitful. . . . Remain in me, and I will remain in you. No branch can bear fruit by itself; it must remain in the vine. Neither can you bear fruit unless you remain in me" (John 15:1-2,4).

Jesus describes Himself as the true vine. The nation of Israel is also called a vine (Isaiah 5:1-7), but Israel was unfaithful to God, yielding only bad fruit. In contrast, Jesus is the faithful and genuine vine, producing good fruit through the branches. And who are those branches? All believers, for all have been called to be spiritually productive in life.

And how does God increase the believer's spiritual productivity? By pruning. This is the responsibility of the Father. But notice who the Father prunes: "every branch that does bear fruit he prunes." These are not Christians who have rebelled against God. They are not trying to see how far they can go with their Christian freedom before they get their hands slapped. They are people who love the Lord, who are already spiritually fruitful and who desire to do His will.

Then why the pruning? Jesus answers that question by saying, "So that it will be even more fruitful" (John 15:2). To further explain the analogy, let me share an experience I had while living in Fresno, California.

In our back yard we had various kinds of fruit trees. A friend who was an amateur horticulturist visited us one afternoon, so I proudly showed him my peach tree, which was loaded with small peaches. He looked at it with the eye of an inspector, and asked with a smile, "Pastor, do you want large peaches from this tree?" I replied, "Certainly I do. At least that's what I'm hoping for." He continued, "Well, you'll never get them by letting all those little peaches hang there. Let me prune the tree for you and I guarantee you'll have all the large peaches you'll be able to eat." I told him to go ahead and prune. In dismay I stood back and watched.

Kale began to shake the tree vigorously and the peaches fell like snow in a Minnesota winter. He even picked several peaches that didn't fall. I yelled, "Wait a minute, Kale. You're ruining my tree. I won't have anything left by the time you get finished." He responded, "It's the only way, Pastor. Your tree won't produce what you really want unless I get rid of more peaches." Well, he was right. That year we had the largest, juiciest, most delicious peaches we have ever had, thanks to someone who knew how to prune effectively.

So what does that have to do with you and me? Everything! Our Father in heaven sees us something like that peach tree. We are producing peaches, but they lack quality. God wants us to be more fruitful in our Christian lives, not only in the sense of quantity, but also in quality. Therefore, He prunes us. But what does God have to prune from our lives? I can't answer that question for each reader, but I will tell about some excess baggage I was carrying in my Christian experience.

Before entering the waiting room, my ministry had been in what some would describe as the fast lane. I had been pastor of a church with over 2000 attenders, had a radio ministry in several states across the country, had traveled throughout the country speaking for churches, retreats, Bible conferences, seminars, and a number of colleges and seminaries. I had earned a doctoral degree, authored thirteen books, and at the time was pastoring another church with an attendance of over 2000. I realized that any success I had achieved was the direct result of the Holy Spirit working in my life. I didn't feel boastful or cocky. Yet there remained an unhealthy attitude of *self-sufficiency* that God needed to prune. In fact, when I first went to my new ministry in Minnesota, I expected to rely on my past experiences and strengths to achieve there what I had accomplished in past ministries.

Another area that needed pruning was my *focus*. Though I had started my two previous ministries with a focus on the local church, to which the Lord had called me, I felt the strong undertow of directing my energies toward personal pursuits in ministry: outside speaking and writing. Such pursuits in themselves were not wrong, but I felt I was neglecting my first responsibility: the local church. That focus also needed pruning.

The Lord also wanted to tenderize me. He needed to prune a "toughness" out of my heart—a type of insensitive spirit. It's not that I didn't care about people's hurts and problems. Rather, I was just preoccupied with what I was doing in my life and ministry. God wanted me to learn how to empathize with those who were hurting.

He also needed to prune what I call "the success syndrome" from my life. Since entering the ministry in 1964, I had never experienced a major failure. Three years as a Christian education director proved to be challenging and fruitful. In fact, I continue to have contact today with some of the disciples resulting from that ministry. Then nearly five years pastoring a church in Winnipeg, Canada, offered another fruitful season of my life. I had the opportunity to develop my preaching ability and learn the basics of pastoring a young congregation. We built a gymnasium and an educational facility on the site and remodeled our old sanctuary. It was quite an enjoyable experience.

That ministry was followed by a successful pastorate in Fresno, California, where I had the opportunity to be part of a church growth process that went from an attendance of 175 to 2300 over a period of thirteen years. We were in a building program almost every other year. Eventually, we built a beautiful 1000-seat sanctuary, and in a few years were back to three Sunday morning services.

Success had become a way of life and an expectation for me. Though I was not giving myself credit for the prosperity in ministry that the Lord continued to bring, I was expecting to just move on to bigger and better things. When the Lord directed me to a church in Minneapolis, Minnesota, my expectations were fully realized. The church had a three-million-dollar budget, a staff of fifty-seven, a large facility, and an opportunity to work with men who were the movers and shakers in business and the Christian world. That was the setting where God pruned the success syndrome from my life.

God may be in the process of pruning something out of your life at this very moment. If this is the case, don't fight it. Instead, welcome it, for His pruning will make you more fruitful and bring greater glory to the Father. As Jesus said, "This is to my Father's glory, that you bear much fruit, showing yourselves to be my disciples" (John 15:8). By illustration, consider two spiritual stalwarts whom God pruned for greater fruitbearing.

JOB: THE PRIESTLY PARENT

Job was a priestly parent because he continually prayed on behalf of his children, even when they were grown and living away from home (Job 1:4-5). The account of Job's great testing describes a man who, in a short period of time, lost his wealth, his children, and his health. And in the months that followed, Job experienced God's waiting room, which was a mere pile of ashes (Job 2:8).

No one knows how long Job endured his misery. But while he waited, his friends only made matters worse by telling him that he must have caused all his problems by sinning. One of his friends counseled, "Blessed is the man whom God corrects; so do not despise the discipline of the Almighty" (Job 5:17). They were convinced that Job's waiting room experience was a result of God's discipline for some sin. Instead of being a comfort to Job, they became a thorn in his side.

Job responded with great anguish of heart, crying, "A despairing man should have the devotion of his friends, even though he forsakes the fear of the Almighty. But my brothers are as undependable as intermittent streams, as the streams that overflow when darkened by thawing ice and swollen with melting snow, but that cease to flow in the dry season, and in the heat vanish from their channels" (Job 6:14-17). For Job it was indeed a dry season, and the comfort of his friends vanished. This giant of a righteous sufferer lamented, "Miserable comforters are you all!" (16:2).

Though Job was innocent of the accusations his friends hurled at him, he did have an area that needed pruning. Job felt that because of his blameless life, he should be experiencing a good life, one with few troubles. But now nothing was making any sense. What had he done wrong to deserve such treatment from God? Nothing! But God wanted to bring Job into an even deeper relationship with Him, to give him an understanding of God like he had never known before. So God removed Job's limited understanding and replaced it with a deeper insight into the Person and workings of the Almighty.

Job's personal testimony describes what he learned about the Lord:

Then Job replied to the LORD: "I know that you can do all things [God is all-powerful]; no plan of yours can be thwarted [God is sovereign and does as He pleases]. You asked, 'Who is this that obscures my counsel without knowledge?' [God is all-knowing]. Surely I spoke of things I did not understand, things too wonderful for me to know. You said, 'Listen now, and I will speak; I will question you, and you shall answer me.' My ears had heard of you but now my eyes have seen you. Therefore I despise myself and repent in dust and ashes." (Job 42:1-6)

It is one thing to hear about God's mercy, grace, faithfulness, power, love, etc. But when one experiences the reality of these qualities, he moves from merely hearing to seeing it for himself. Not only did Job benefit from what he learned of God while waiting, but he was also generously rewarded after going through his ordeal:

After Job had prayed for his friends, the LORD made him prosperous again and gave him twice as much as he had before. All his brothers and sisters and everyone who had known him before came and ate with him in his house. They comforted and consoled him over all the trouble the LORD had brought upon him, and each one gave him a piece of silver and a gold ring. The LORD blessed the latter part of Job's life more than the first. (Job 42:10-12)

God restored to Job his family, his health, his wealth, and his friends. Though the process of waiting was painful, riddled with questions, and lonely, the result was wonderfully beneficial. This is not to promote a "wait and get wealthy" attitude. Rather, it's a recognition of God's promise to honor those who wait faithfully on Him. He may honor some with restored peace or renewed relationships and others with material blessings, but one thing is certain: Resting in God is worth the pruning and the waiting process.

JOSEPH: THE PRIME MINISTER OF EGYPT

Another fruitful believer who experienced a waiting period in his life was Joseph. Like Job, this young man Joseph was in God's waiting room as an innocent and obedient servant. Job's waiting room was a pile of ashes, whereas Joseph's was a distant land and a long prison term.

On two occasions as a young man, Joseph received a vision from God. He enthusiastically related those visions to his brothers and father. His brothers hated him because his dreams placed them in a subordinate role to him. They were filled with jealousy and plotted to kill him. But with the intervention of the oldest brother, Reuben, they decided to spare his life, and then later sold him to a caravan of Midianite merchants headed toward Egypt.

At first everything seemed to go smoothly for young Joseph. Even though he was sold as a slave to Potiphar, the captain of the guard, the Lord made certain that Joseph prospered in everything he did. Potiphar put Joseph in charge of his household and entrusted to his care everything he owned.

Enter Potiphar's wife, who attempted to seduce the Hebrew slave. Joseph refused her advances. Then one day he happened to be alone in the house. When the captain's wife sized up the situation, she seized the opportunity and grabbed Joseph's cloak and begged him to make love to her. Joseph fled from the room, but she had his cloak in her hands. When her husband returned to the house, she con-

cocted a story about Joseph trying to seduce her. Understandably, Potiphar became furious and threw Joseph into
prison. The length of his prison term is unknown, but the
facts indicate that he spent an extra two years in prison
because an inmate forgot to mention Joseph to the king
after being released from prison (Genesis 40:14-15,23).

The Scriptures are also silent regarding defects in this
young man's life. When Joseph entered his waiting room,
he was not under God's discipline for sin. On the contrary,
he was imprisoned because he refused to sin. So what would
God have to prune from Joseph's life? Perhaps some of his
hostile feelings toward his brothers.

One could imagine how he must have felt toward his
brothers when he was first sold to the Midianite caravan. I
do not believe that Joseph possessed a great knowledge
about God's purpose when he was first taken to Egypt.
Perhaps the prison experience, with its isolation, gave him
the time and opportunity to think through everything. It was
probably while in prison that Joseph developed his understanding of God and began to see the pieces of the mosaic
formulate into a beautiful pattern. So, as God pruned away
some of those natural feelings of anger and bitterness
against his brothers, Joseph gained a new insight into the
character and purpose of God.

After Joseph told his brothers who he was, he gave
them a short theology lesson about God's character and
purpose. He said, "Do not be distressed and do not be angry
with yourselves for selling me here, because it was to save
lives that God sent me ahead of you. For two years now
there has been famine in the land, and for the next five
years there will not be plowing and reaping. But God sent
me ahead of you to preserve for you a remnant on earth and
to save your lives by a great deliverance. So then, it was not
you who sent me here, but God" (Genesis 45:5-8).

Those are powerful words coming from the lips of one who had been abused by his brothers, especially when he was in a position to take advantage of the situation. He could have easily gotten even with them for what they had done to him. But Joseph was able to see beyond their evil intentions and capture an understanding of God's sovereign purpose. His brothers had an evil motive, stemming from jealousy, but God had His own agenda. The Lord allowed Joseph's brothers to carry out their scheme and worked it into His greater purpose.

After the death of their father Jacob, the brothers feared for their lives. They thought that perhaps Joseph was being kind to them simply for the sake of their father. So they came to him once again in deep humility to apologize for what they had done to him. But Joseph replied, "You intended to harm me, but God intended it for good to accomplish what is now being done, the saving of many lives" (Genesis 50:20).

As I observed closely Joseph's response to his circumstances, I was greatly encouraged by what I saw there. I felt that if God could use the evil intentions of Joseph's brothers to accomplish a greater purpose in the life of his family, the Lord could do the same for me by using the schemes of those who wanted a leadership change at my church. I concluded that my responsibility was not to seek revenge, but rather to allow the Lord to work out His purpose in His time.

Are you the victim of someone's abuse? Jealousy? Anger? Misunderstanding? The Lord may give you the opportunity to repay your adversaries. If He does, remember Joseph's response: "You intended to harm me, but God intended it for good. . . ." Perhaps you feel like both Job and Joseph. You are not guilty of some terrible sin. You have been walking closely with the Lord and constantly enjoy His presence. As far as you know, you are living in obedience to His revealed will stated in Scripture.

However, you are also facing a seemingly insurmountable problem. You've been agonizing over the issue and have now come to realize that you have just entered God's waiting room. Don't despair. Though the end may not yet be in sight, be assured that there *will* be an end. One day you will be leaving this waiting period, and those little pieces of the puzzle will begin to fit together. You'll be able to look back on this experience and say with David, "You turned my wailing into dancing; you removed my sackcloth and clothed me with joy, that my heart may sing to you and not be silent. O LORD my God, I will give you thanks forever" (Psalm 30:11-12).

As I close this chapter, I want to leave you with four thoughts, beginning with the process of waiting. The process of waiting is not a pleasant one. Job was in pain while he sat on the ash heap. And Joseph agonized as he sat in prison. But in spite of the pain, God's waiting room experience is well worth the suffering. God uses the whole ordeal to make us more fruitful in our personal life and more mature in our character. God does not promise greater wealth, as in the case of Job, or greater prestige, which Joseph experienced. But He does promise a better life. We may again identify with David, who wrote, "Weeping may remain for a night, but rejoicing comes in the morning" (Psalm 30:5).

Secondly, God may be in the process of pruning something from your life. It may be an attitude of self-sufficiency, pride, the success syndrome, a wrong focus, or even some negative feeling that you have toward someone. Perhaps you've been hurt by a friend or an acquaintance, intentionally or unintentionally. You feel anger, resentment, hostility. It's eating away at you and affecting you in a negative way. Why not let the Lord take that out of your life? Whatever He brings to your mind to be pruned, let Him do it. Ask Him to cut it out of your life as a surgeon would remove a cancerous growth. You don't need it. You'll live better without it.

Another thought to reflect on is that God will take care of the problem people in your life. If someone is giving you a lot of headaches, turn him over to the Lord. God is an expert at handling the opposition. Remember, they are answerable to Him and you are responsible for how you react to such individuals. Keep your conscience clear, your heart pure, and your hands clean. If you know that you stand in a right relationship with God, then be assured that He will reward you accordingly. The psalmist penned these words of testimony: "The LORD has dealt with me according to my righteousness; according to the cleanness of my hands he has rewarded me" (Psalm 18:20). You, too, will be rewarded.

One final consideration: You may not be in God's waiting room right at this moment. In fact, you may not enter it for years. Hence, what I am saying may not apply to you at the present. But I have little doubt that what you read in these pages will be excellent preparation if God gives you the privilege of entering His waiting room. In the meantime, you'll have something to share with your friends who wonder where to turn as they go through the crucible of waiting for God's next chapter in their lives.

2
The Discipline of Waiting

I grew up in a row house in Lancaster, Pennsylvania. The rooms were quite small, though when I was a child they seemed large. Between the kitchen and the family room hung a yardstick sometimes used for measuring and other times as an instrument of correction. I don't know why my parents decided to use a yardstick, but it served its purpose well. Whenever we passed from the kitchen into the family room we were reminded of our parents' values and the penalty for violating them.

I became quite familiar with the impact of that yardstick. I've been told that I was quite a tease in my younger years, and I know that neither of my sisters appreciated my foolishness. When I indulged in making life miserable for them, they were quick to inform Mom and Dad, who did not delay to carry out the needed discipline. When the time arrived for my discipline, I would have to remove the yardstick from the wall, hand it to one of my parents, and then bend over for the memorable impression.

Later in life, when I first came across the book of Hebrews, I had little difficulty understanding the meaning of the words, "No discipline seems pleasant at the time, but painful" (Hebrews 12:11). I understood the pain. It was the same kind of pain I experienced numerous times in grade school, and even once when I was in ninth grade, thanks to a shop teacher who had tired of my excuses for continually forgetting to bring my class project to school. I felt the pain on my backside, on my hands, and even on my ears. I didn't like it, but never questioned that I deserved every smack I received, and many that I never did receive.

As I began to grow in my Christian life, I saw several parallels between God disciplining me and my parents' chastening process. That's what the writer to the Hebrews uses to illustrate a point. He writes, "In your struggle against sin, you have not yet resisted to the point of shedding your blood. And you have forgotten that word of encouragement that addresses you as sons: 'My son, do not make light of the Lord's discipline, and do not lose heart when he rebukes you, because the Lord disciplines those he loves, and he punishes everyone he accepts as a son'" (Hebrews 12:4-6).

WHAT IS CHASTENING?

The Greek word translated "discipline" in the NIV and "chasten" in the KJV is *paideuo*, primarily denoting the training of children and suggesting the broad idea of education. For instance, "Moses was *educated* in all the wisdom of the Egyptians and was powerful in speech and action" (Acts 7:22). But it also implies that some of the training is achieved through affliction: "Endure hardship as discipline; God is treating you as sons. For what son is not disciplined by his father?" (Hebrews 12:7). Therefore, we need to see the *purpose* of discipline or chastening as positive, although the *process* of discipline may be negative. No one enjoys the process, but as he understands discipline properly, it will be easier to accept.

For instance, the writer to the Hebrews concludes that *discipline provides evidence that you belong to God*: "If you are not disciplined (and everyone undergoes discipline), then you are illegitimate children and not true sons" (Hebrews 12:8). When was the last time you disciplined someone else's child? You may have wanted to chasten the little darling as you watched him tear around your home, or listened to him scream in a restaurant. Instead, you controlled your turbulent emotions as you neared the boiling point and settled for a forced smile and an innocent question: "Does he always do that?" You decide against taking any other action because he is not your child.

DISCIPLINE VERSUS PUNISHMENT

In the same way, the Lord *disciplines* only those who belong to Him, but He *punishes* those who are not His. The difference between discipline and punishment lies primarily in the purpose of what God does. The process may be similar in either case, but the purpose is radically different.

The Scriptures offer two reasons for God's discipline and one for His punishment. First, He disciplines because He wants to prevent the believer, His child, from getting into trouble and hurting himself. He also disciplines because the believer needs to make some major changes in his life. When the Lord observes a significant problem in the Christian's attitude or behavior, He designs a plan to correct that fault. In both cases, discipline is for the believer's good.

In contrast, God punishes the unbeliever for one

major reason: sin. God's address to the spiritual leaders of Israel announced an impending judgment:

> "Woe to the shepherds who are destroying and scattering the sheep of my pasture!" declares the LORD. Therefore this is what the LORD, the God of Israel, says to the shepherds who tend my people: "Because you have scattered my flock and driven them away and have not bestowed care on them, I will bestow punishment on you for the evil you have done," declares the LORD. (Jeremiah 23:1-2)

While discipline may include affliction for the purposes of prevention or correction, punishment is for the purpose of executing a penalty for sin.

Discipline is also good in that it provides evidence of God's love. When you are being disciplined, you may think God really dislikes you to permit such severe consequences to crash in on you. But discipline is not a sign of God's hatred. It is rather an evidence of His love. In fact, the Bible openly declares that "he who spares the rod hates his son, but he who loves him is careful to discipline him" (Proverbs 13:24).

As a parent, you always want the best for your child. Not wanting him to get hurt, you establish parameters and provide guidelines of safety in order to protect him from unnecessary trouble. The child is taught values and priorities. By word and example, you communicate the difference between right and wrong. You understand your child better than he thinks you do because you've watched him develop. You know his strengths and weaknesses. You understand the areas in which he will probably be most tempted. You inform him what behavior is not acceptable and which choices should be avoided at all costs. When your child violates those parameters, you take action to correct the problem because you love your child.

God responds in a similar manner. If He didn't love you, He'd let you do whatever you want. He would have no pity when you paint yourself into a corner and would ignore you when you fall flat on your face. But that is not how the God of Scripture reacts to His own. He does everything possible to keep you out of trouble. Sometimes that requires discipline.

To better understand this idea, let's take a look at two types of discipline that the Lord uses: (1) *preventive discipline* and (2) *corrective discipline*. Usually when we think about discipline, we consider only the corrective type. But let's first look at preventive discipline.

PREVENTIVE DISCIPLINE

Preventive discipline is not an affliction resulting from sin, but rather *a facilitator to help the believer turn away from sin.* The psalmist testified, "It was good for me to be afflicted so that I might learn your decrees . . . . I know, O LORD, that your laws are righteous, and in faithfulness you have afflicted me" (Psalm 119:71,75). God sometimes assails His beloved saints to prevent some potential sin. Consider the apostle Paul, a prime candidate for preventive discipline.

Few believers have ever walked as closely with the Lord as Paul. He confirmed his commitment to the Lord with these words: "To me, to live is Christ and to die is gain" (Philippians 1:21). The essence of his life was Jesus Christ, and yet he suffered. Why? He disclosed the reason to the believers living in Corinth.

Paul portrayed a baffling personal event to his readers, possibly an "out of the body" experience. He described a man who was taken up into "the third heaven" and witnessed sights so extraordinary that the human mind would fail in its struggle to grasp them. Paul was not authorized to recount what he saw. Such an unprecedented experience might have enticed the apostle toward excessive pride, thus hindering his effectiveness for Christ. But Paul elaborated on the purpose of God's discipline: "To keep me from becoming conceited because of these surpassingly great revelations, there was given me a thorn in my flesh, a messenger of Satan, to torment me" (2 Corinthians 12:7).

As in the case of Job, Paul's affliction resulted from Satanic activity. However, Satan did not personally confront Paul. Instead, he used one of his demons or messengers to torment him. And though God may indeed allow the forces of darkness to administer suffering on a believer, every demon is under God's authority and cannot move beyond the Lord's permissive will.

The apostle did not disclose the specific identity of his "thorn in the flesh," so we are left to speculate. Many Bible scholars believe it was a physical affliction such as an eye disorder. Others feel it might have been an emotional ailment. Whatever it might have been, the malady was a major aggravation to Paul. He anguished so greatly from his problem that he asked the Lord on three occasions to withdraw the irritant (2 Corinthians 12:8). But the Lord declined.

One might surmise that either Paul did not pray in faith or that God was powerless to heal him of the affliction, but neither was the case. On more than one occasion God used Paul to heal others. God could certainly have removed the adversity in Paul's case, but chose not to. Instead, the Lord encouraged the apostle by promising, "My grace is sufficient for you, for my power is made perfect in weakness" (2 Corinthians 12:9). In other words, God gave Paul a lifelong problem in order to help him rivet his eyes on the Lord rather than on his own experiences. Paul's boasting was to be in the Lord, not in the special effects he encountered while in the third heaven.

Hence, the apostle entered God's waiting room for an undetermined period of time. It commenced when the demon first attacked him, but ended when God made it transparent that the "barb" would remain, but that the grace to endure the affliction would also be constant.

This raises an important principle. Our afflictions usually come and go. Though weeks, months, and even years may pass, eventually the problem dissipates and we move on in our lives. However, at other times an affliction enters our lives and persists indefinitely. We may do everything in our power to expel the crisis—including prayer. Nevertheless, God may counter with, "My grace is sufficient for you, for my power is made perfect in weakness" (2 Corinthians 12:9). That is not the answer we want to hear. We don't wish any negative intrusion of a permanent nature into our lives. But the choice between permanence and transience is not always ours to make. Instead, our choice may be limited to whether we accept the inevitable or reject it; whether we embrace God's sufficient grace or just grin and bear it.

Paul chose to acquiesce to the permanence of his affliction. Then he embraced God's sufficient grace so that he could live with it. He testified, "Therefore I will boast all the more gladly about my weaknesses, so that Christ's power may rest on me. That is why, for Christ's sake, I delight in weaknesses, in insults, in hardships, in persecutions, in difficulties. For when I am weak, then I am strong" (2 Corinthians 12:9-10).

Personally, I have found this principle to be true in my own life. Some of my most powerful messages have been delivered when I was physically or emotionally exhausted and completely dependent on the Lord. It was during some of these most difficult periods of life that God's grace and strength penetrated my life to the point where I amazed myself with exceptional calmness and clarity of thought.

Recently, a very close friend of ours lost her husband at the age of fifty-four. His sudden death sent shock waves throughout the church he attended and his place of employment. When I called Jewel, I was expecting to give some special words of comfort and encouragement, but instead, I was a recipient of God's grace to her. She explained how the Lord had prepared her sons and herself for this tragedy. She related how she had sensed the prayers of all her friends and how the Lord had given special strength and well-rooted peace as she went through the process of making funeral arrangements and contacting family members.

Obviously, my friend's loss was of a permanent nature. But how can one know for certain whether an affliction will be permanent or temporary? What rule of thumb can we use to decide whether we should continue to pray for God's deliverance from the predicament or for His grace to endure the ordeal?

In the case of some physical afflictions, the prognosis can be known through medical examination. However, in other cases you may not know for a longer period of time. I have made it a practice to continue praying for a change until the Lord makes it known to me that the condition is permanent. I'll speak more about how to discern God's will in Chapter 9.

CORRECTIVE DISCIPLINE

As we have just seen, God uses a preventive kind of discipline on people who are walking closely with Him, perhaps to protect them from a temptation beyond their ability to resist. Now let's investigate the other kind of discipline God uses, which is corrective in purpose.

Jonah was a perfect candidate for corrective discipline. This prophet's name went down in history because of his act of disobedience. He explicitly knew the will of God. God's communication to the prophet was clear: "Go to the great city of Nineveh and preach against it, because its wickedness has come up before me" (Jonah 1:2). But Jonah ran away from the Lord and headed in the opposite direction from Nineveh for a city named Tarshish.

Jonah fathomed neither God's character nor His nature, even though he was one of the Lord's gifted prophets. He surmised that he could somehow hide from God. Either he never read or he would not accept David's perspective of God's omnipresence (His presence everywhere simultaneously) in Psalm 139:

> Where can I go from your Spirit? Where can I flee from your presence? If I go up to the heavens, you are there; if I make my bed in the depths, you are there. If I rise on the wings of the dawn, if I settle on the far side of the sea, even there your hand will guide me, your right hand will hold me fast. If I say, "Surely the darkness will hide me and the light become night around me," even the darkness will not be dark to you; the night will shine like the day, for darkness is as light to you. (Psalm 139:7-12)

Because he thought he could hide from the Lord, Jonah wasted a lot of time getting himself and others into trouble (Jonah 1:4-14). When a person sins against God, not only does he hurt himself, but he inevitably hurts others, especially those who are closest to him. King David was a man who had a high profile. And when he sinned, the consequences reached far beyond himself. After David's affair with Bathsheba, God sent the prophet Nathan to him with this ominous message from the Lord:

> "Now, therefore, the sword will never depart from your house, because you despised me and took the wife of Uriah the Hittite to be your own. . . . Out of your own household I am going to bring calamity upon you. Before your very eyes I will take your wives and give them to one who is close to you, and he will lie with your wives in broad daylight. You did it in secret, but I will do this thing in broad daylight before all Israel." (2 Samuel 12:10-12)

After David repented of his sin, Nathan countered with these words: "The LORD has taken away your sin. You are not going to die. But because by doing this you have made the enemies of the LORD show utter contempt, the son born to you will die" (2 Samuel 12:13-14).

What happened to David has been repeated time and again in our own generation. We may do our own thing in secret, but the consequences of our actions will eventually creep out of the closet and into the public arena. And the higher the profile of the offender, the more public his offense.

Jonah hoped to flee from the presence of God. But his rebellion almost cost the lives of the entire crew aboard ship. After being out on the sea for a few days, the sailors experienced an enormous storm. The gale winds that were vehemently ravaging the ship convinced the crew that death and destruction were inevitable. They did everything in their power to avoid the damage, but their efforts proved futile. They cast lots to discover who was responsible for the storm and the lot fell on Jonah. The prophet admitted the storm was God's discipline for his rebellion. He explained that the only way to save the ship and themselves was to throw him overboard.

When they finally agreed to his solution, Jonah entered God's waiting room, located in the stomach of a large fish. As he rolled around in the gastric juices of the fish's stomach, Jonah responded to God's discipline. He repented of his sin and asked the Lord for a second chance. The prophet later testified of God's grace and mercy:

> "In my distress I called to the LORD, and he an-
> swered me. From the depths of the grave I called for
> help, and you listened to my cry. . . . When my life
> was ebbing away, I remembered you, LORD, and my
> prayer rose to you, to your holy temple. Those who
> cling to worthless idols forfeit the grace that could be
> theirs. But I, with a song of thanksgiving, will sacri-
> fice to you. What I have vowed I will make good. Sal-
> vation comes from the LORD." (Jonah 2:2,7-9)

He apparently promised to obey the Lord by carrying the message to Nineveh because when the fish spewed Jonah onto the land, he walked throughout the great city and preached repentance.

Some people enter God's waiting room out of a rebellious spirit. That room may be a drug rehabilitation center, a psychiatric ward in a hospital, a courtroom, a bed of affliction, a financially entangled mess, or some other undesirable condition or place. Even when an individual is in God's waiting room because he wants to run his own life and keep God at a distance, there is still a way out.

That open door begins with *remorse.* It is not uncommon for a husband to feel distress when he has cheated on his wife. He knows he has violated her trust in him. He feels guilty, perhaps even unworthy of her love. Sorrow may grip his soul. Likewise, when we sin against God, we have been unfaithful to Him and have violated His trust in us. If one is not truly contrite for what he has done, it is doubtful that he understands sin. When remorse does surface, it needs to emerge from recognition of sin and not from the fact that he got caught.

From remorse, one then moves into *confession.* The word *confess* means to agree with God that I have sinned against Him. Many people limit their confession to mere lip service. Others play a semantics game and camouflage sin with words like "fault" or "mistake." Or they metamorphose sexual immorality until it is transformed to emerge as an "unwise relationship." But true confession implies a denouncement of sin because it violates the holy character of God.

The next step is to *repent* of that sin. To repent means to change one's mind. One must admit that what he has done is wrong and determine in his heart that he does not want to repeat the offense. David not only spoke the words "I have sinned against the LORD" (2 Samuel 12:13), but he also sought God's cleansing and a change of heart:

> Have mercy on me, O God, according to your unfailing love; according to your great compassion blot out my transgressions. Wash away all my iniquity and cleanse me from my sin. For I know my transgressions, and my sin is always before me. Against you, you only, have I sinned and done what is evil in your sight, so that you are proved right when you speak and justified when you judge. . . . Create in me a pure heart, O God, and renew a steadfast spirit within me. . . . Restore to me the joy of your salvation and grant me a willing spirit, to sustain me. (Psalm 51:1-4,10,12)

Today confession has been cheapened by surface admissions of guilt, followed quickly by justification for the sin or by the rationalization that all of us sin. The implication is this: "It's true that I've made this mistake, but who doesn't make mistakes at one time or another? So you should forgive me and not discipline me in any way." Jesus' words to the adulteress too often become a convenient way to cover up the ugliness of our sin.

The final response to God's corrective discipline should be a willingness to make *restitution* wherever possible. David continued with his prayer by saying, "Then I will teach transgressors your ways, and sinners will turn back to you. Save me from bloodguilt, O God, the God who saves me, and my tongue will sing of your righteousness. O Lord, open my lips, and my mouth will declare your praise" (Psalm 51:13-15). David wanted a changed life. He wanted to use the rest of his days to proclaim God's love and mercy, and so he rejected the pleasures of sin.

Once these steps have been followed, the disciplined believer should then be *restored* to fellowship. However, if the individual has been involved in a public ministry, it would be wise to include a waiting period before he or she renews that service. Restoration to fellowship should be quick, but restoration to ministry needs to occur more slowly. Time is needed to heal hurts, build trust, and observe a renewed lifestyle and commitment to God.

The Lord does not take any more delight in disciplining His children than we do in disciplining our own children. But sometimes we, like our children, misbehave and need to learn obedience. This means that we must humbly place ourselves under His authority and stop playing religious games. The Lord isn't waiting for us to mouth a few words of sorrow. He wants to see action. He seeks evidence that we mean business with Him.

REFLECTIONS

If you have been walking closely with the Lord but are now experiencing His waiting room, it may be for one of two reasons. He may be in the process of *pruning* some areas of your life so that you will become more fruitful. To see whether this is the case, check your relationship with the Lord. If you have peace in your heart that you have been pleasing Him, then accept His pruning process. When God prunes, He not only takes the unnecessary away, but also replaces it with better quality.

On the other hand, the Lord may have positioned you in His waiting room because He sees *a potential problem* arising in your life. If He allows you to continue the way you are going, you may face a temptation that could entice you to the point of yielding, resulting in an ineffective Christian walk and witness. Therefore, God may be taking you through a preventive discipline process. You may later be able to handle the responsibility, the honor, or the pressure you cannot handle at this point. Therefore, He is allowing you to experience affliction so that He can teach you what you need to know and add to whatever is lacking in your life. You will then be able to identify with Isaiah, who wrote, "This is what the LORD says—your Redeemer, the Holy One of Israel: 'I am the LORD your God, who teaches you what is best for you, who directs you in the way you should go'" (Isaiah 48:17). If this is the case, then wait patiently for the Lord to complete what He has begun.

The third possible reason God may have brought you into His waiting room is *if you have taken matters into your own hands* and have decided to run life your way. You may still be attending church, teaching Sunday school, or singing in the choir. You may be active in doing the Lord's work, like Jonah the prophet. But inside there may be a rebellious spirit that does not want to be under anyone's authority. You enjoy God's Word as long as it doesn't interfere with your personal plans or lifestyle. You may even have a lot of Christian friends you enjoy as long as they don't point out any areas of your life that need to change. Or you are willing to serve in various capacities as long as people do things your way and march to the beat of your drum.

This lifestyle God will not accept. And if it continues, He may call you into His waiting room as a place of corrective discipline. There you will remain until He feels you have truly confessed your sin, repented of your sin, and are willing to demonstrate a life of repentance and humility.

Whatever the reason we may enter His room, He promises to be there with us. He guarantees, "Never will I leave you; never will I forsake you" (Hebrews 13:5). Some will be able to exit His waiting room by turning their lives over to Him. Others will remain there until the Lord has completed His purpose. But all who wait upon the Lord "will renew their strength. They will soar on wings like eagles; they will run and not grow weary, they will walk and not be faint" (Isaiah 40:31).

3

Confronting Your Doubts

Mr. Axelson and his wife were driving to their Minnesota cabin for the weekend. They had just come from celebrating his retirement from the headquarters of the Evangelical Free Church in Minneapolis. It was to be a weekend spent with some of their grown children, where they could continue the gala affair. But as Mr. and Mrs. Axelson were headed north to the cabin, the car suddenly veered off the road and down an embankment. Mr. Axelson received painful but not serious injuries. However, his wife's injuries were far more serious, and the recovery has been both slow and limited.

Couldn't the Lord have prevented that accident? Why would He allow a tragedy of this nature to strike such committed servants? And why now, just after retirement? This was the time of life they had both so eagerly anticipated. The days ahead were supposed to be filled with good, not evil; laughter, not sorrow. But a disaster marred those plans.

One of the most natural responses to hard times is to question, and possibly even to doubt. We speculate, "Does God know what is happening in my life? Is He able to do anything about what is going on? How could this have happened to me? When will it be over? Will I ever recover from this experience?"

Questions, objections, and protests harass our minds about the future, about people, about ourselves and about God. And we're not alone in our confusion. The Scriptures furnish many examples of others who questioned the justice, the logic, or the purpose of their burdens.

Listen to the plight of one who was unjustly accused. He cried to God, "O God, whom I praise, do not remain silent, for wicked and deceitful men have opened their mouths against me; they have spoken against me with lying tongues. With words of hatred they surround me; they attack me without cause. In return for my friendship they accuse me, but I am a man of prayer. They repay me evil for good, and hatred for my friendship" (Psalm 109:1-5). These were the exposed wounds of David, who was described by the prophet Samuel as "a man after [God's] own heart" (1 Samuel 13:14). He was misunderstood, hated for no reason, and hunted like a fugitive by a jealous king. Why? What was God trying to accomplish? David did not always find the answers to all his questions.

Another cry poured from the lips of Moses, who could not understand why God would give him the overwhelming responsibility of managing close to three million people who didn't want to be under anyone's authority. He questioned God:

> "Why have you brought this trouble on your servant? What have I done to displease you that you put the burden of all these people on me? Did I conceive all

these people? Did I give them birth? Why do you tell me to carry them in my arms, as a nurse carries an infant, to the land you promised on oath to their forefathers? Where can I get meat for all these people? They keep wailing to me, 'Give us meat to eat!' I cannot carry all these people by myself; the burden is too heavy for me." (Numbers 11:11-14)

In spite of all the miracles God had performed through Moses, the lawgiver remained puzzled by the ways of God.

Then there were the Israelites themselves, who complained more than once, doubting God's ability to meet their needs and Moses' ability to lead them. When they lacked food, they complained to Moses, "If only we had died by the LORD's hand in Egypt! There we sat around pots of meat and ate all the food we wanted, but you have brought us out into this desert to starve this entire assembly to death" (Exodus 16:3). Later they grumbled when they lacked water, complaining, "Why did you bring us up out of Egypt to make us and our children and livestock die of thirst?" (Exodus 17:3).

They were convinced further that God never sent Moses in the first place, so they criticized Moses and Aaron:

"You have gone too far! The whole community is holy, every one of them, and the LORD is with them. Why then do you set yourselves above the LORD's assembly? . . . Isn't it enough that you have brought us up out of a land flowing with milk and honey to kill us in the desert? And now you also want to lord it over us? Moreover, you haven't brought us into a land flowing with milk and honey or given us an inheritance of fields and vineyards." (Numbers 16:3,13-14)

Whether it was with David, Moses, or Israel, God's ways were often mysterious, confusing to the finite mind, raising questions that sometimes led to doubt.

Today we still question. We fret. We find it difficult to believe that God is still in control, working out His purpose. And this causes us to doubt. But what is doubting?

WHAT IS MEANT BY "DOUBTING"?

You've heard the expression "doubting Thomas," which comes from the encounter Thomas had with the other disciples soon after Jesus' resurrection. Thomas did not believe that Jesus had risen from the dead. He expressed his doubt when he told the other disciples, "Unless I see the nail marks in his hands and put my finger where the nails were, and put my hand into his side, I will not believe it" (John 20:25). In other words, Thomas was telling the others, "Seeing is believing." Without actually seeing the evidence with his eyes, Thomas would not believe.

I can easily identify with Thomas. More than once I fixed my eyes in search of evidence that God was at work on a problem that I faced. But as I examined the circumstances, the data failed to verify God's presence and His work. At times like those, I've had to change my focus to the facts presented in God's Word, such as "I will never leave you nor forsake you" (Joshua 1:5) or "As the heavens are higher than the earth, so are my ways higher than your ways and my thoughts than your thoughts" (Isaiah 55:9). Though I could not see the "whys," the "what ifs," and the "what nows," I had to make a choice to either believe what God had told me in His Word, or to reject what He had revealed there.

Jesus' response to Thomas was, "Stop doubting and believe. . . . Because you have seen me, you have believed;

blessed are those who have not seen and yet have believed" (John 20:27,29). God doesn't tell us to live by blind faith. Through the Scriptures, through our personal experiences, and through His work in the lives of others, God has provided all the evidence we need to believe and not to doubt. But in spite of all the confirmation, doubts still do arise and can lead us to sin against God. And that raises another question.

ARE ALL DOUBTS SINFUL?

Recently my wife and I were having a discussion about doubts. She asked, "Honey, have you ever questioned God's leading us to minister at Orange?" I pondered her question for a while and then replied, "No. There has never been a doubt in my mind concerning any of the ministries to which the Lord has led us. However, I do have emotional fluctuations at times and have to go back to the fact that I am where I am supposed to be. So I have to adjust my feelings to the facts, and not vice versa."

You may also have emotional highs and lows when you are going through an adjustment period in life, so it is important to distinguish between a mental doubt and an emotional fluctuation. With a doubt, you may be questioning the Lord's character, purpose, or ability. However, when your emotions bounce around from one extreme to the next, you are not necessarily doubting God, but rather thinking, "I know He is in control and knows what He is doing, but I am too emotionally drained to even think straight." The entire time I ministered in Minnesota, I never doubted that God had led me there and sustained me through the difficulties. But my emotions experienced many highs and lows within a twenty-four hour period.

However, doubts do surface. You may truly wonder

how much God knows what is going on and to what extent He either can make a change or will affect the situation. Do we sin against the Lord whenever doubts pass through our minds? Absolutely not. The sin is not in the thoughts that enter our minds. On the other hand, when we allow those thoughts to so grip our minds that we replace God's truth with circumstantial evidence, then we are on dangerous grounds of doubting.

For instance, Jesus said, "You have heard that it was said, 'Do not commit adultery.' But I tell you that anyone who looks at a woman lustfully has already committed adultery with her in his heart" (Matthew 5:27-28). The sin is not the look, but rather it is the lust. You cannot escape fleeting thoughts that will enter your mind at different times, but you can prevent them from controlling your mind and your actions. As someone said, "You can't keep the birds from flying overhead, but you can prevent them from building a nest in your hair."

When you are confronted by difficult circumstances, you will naturally feel anxiety, experience a degree of fear, and discover that doubts have entered your mind. The question to address at that point is, "Am I going to be controlled by my doubts or will I entrust the situation into the Lord's hands, allowing Him to dispel my doubts?" Even though what you encounter is unjust, illogical, and difficult to understand, you must make a choice. You can choose to turn over the situation to the Lord so that He can complete what has been started. Or you may choose to reject what He has revealed in Scripture and wallow in the distressing circumstances.

Sometimes we just need to understand more about the source of our doubts. In many cases we would be far less doubtful if we understood where these thoughts originated so that we could deal with them early on.

WHAT CAUSES OUR DOUBTS?

There are many contributing factors to our doubts, but four in particular surface on a regular basis: (1) a wrong focus, (2) a lack of experience, (3) misinformation, and (4) ignorance.

When I speak of a *wrong focus*, I'm referring to taking our eyes off the Lord and gazing at our circumstances. Peter fell into this trap when he attempted to walk on water. You remember the occasion. Strong winds had whipped up the waves of the lake the disciples were crossing. Suddenly the disciples looked out on the lake and saw Jesus walking toward them. Observing the terror on the disciples' faces, Jesus attempted to calm them, saying, "Take courage! It is I. Don't be afraid." Peter replied, "Lord, if it's you, tell me to come to you on the water" (Matthew 14:27-28). Jesus told Peter to come. So with fear and trembling, Peter carefully stepped out onto the water and quickly realized that he was indeed standing up.

Like a man walking on a huge waterbed, Peter tried to balance himself on the waves as he inched his way toward the Lord. His emotions completed the cycle from fear to elation and then back to fear again, for he suddenly realized the impossibility of what he was doing. "Man can't walk on water," he thought. "What in the world do I think I'm doing out here? The wind is blasting in my face and I'm getting drenched by the waves slapping against me." Peter was too far away to grab hold of the boat and too over-whelmed by his circumstances to gain victory over his doubts, so he did the only thing he could do: He cried to the Lord for help.

The Bible vividly describes the Lord's response to Peter: "Immediately Jesus reached out his hand and caught him. 'You of little faith,' he said, 'why did you doubt?'"

(Matthew 14:31). Peter was doing so well until he refocused his eyes from the Lord to his circumstances, a response not too uncommon in my own experience. When I've gone through deep waters, I've found myself praising God one moment and then wondering, "Is He really going to get me through this? Will He bring good out of this terrible situation?"

A second contributor to doubting is *lack of experience with the Lord.* For the first nineteen years of my ministry, I experienced few doubts. But as I entered my twentieth year of ministry, I discovered several situations beyond my control, and my bank of wisdom had already been overdrawn. The pressures continually mounted and my uneasiness turned to anxiety, resulting in discouragement and eventually a state of depression, a path I had never traveled before.

I prayed, but could see no evidence of God answering. I talked with some friends, but soon discovered they were limited in the help they could offer. I read and reread many passages of Scripture, but even that did not dispel the anxiety I felt. However, as the Lord sustained me throughout the ordeal, I've concluded that back then He was preparing me for an even more trying period that would last for two years. That two-year testing period would have been devastating had it not been for the earlier three-month conditioning experience. Though doubts about God's faithfulness had arisen during that first testing, they were greatly reduced during the second trial. I knew I could trust the Lord, even though I could not understand what He was doing nor why He was allowing the difficulties to occur.

Another cause for doubting generates from *misinformation.* Some people have been told that if they are truly walking closely with the Lord, they will not experience suffering, great difficulties, or tragedies. They believe that if a believer is confronted by a major problem he must have done something wrong. Faithfulness to God and suffering seem to be incompatible in the minds of some believers.

Job's friends held to that attitude when they accused him, "Is it for your piety that he rebukes you and brings charges against you? Is not your wickedness great? Are not your sins endless?" (Job 22:4-5). Jesus' disciples held to the same opinion when they searched for the reason why a certain man had been blind from birth. They inquired of the Lord, "Rabbi, who sinned, this man or his parents, that he was born blind?" (John 9:2).

As I have studied the Scriptures, I've noticed that almost every servant of the Lord experienced great hardship in his life. In fact, the Scriptures verify that God allows us to experience suffering so that He might develop our character. The apostle Paul, who had his share of problems, wrote this:

> We rejoice in the hope of the glory of God. Not only so, but we also rejoice in our sufferings, because we know that suffering produces perseverance; perseverance, character; and character, hope. And hope does not disappoint us, because God has poured out his love into our hearts by the Holy Spirit, whom he has given us. (Romans 5:2-5)

The fourth reason that doubts enter our hearts and minds is our *ignorance* of God's character, purposes, ability, and past works. Difficulties drive me to the Scriptures so that I can find answers to my questions. I want to see how others handled their problems. I crave to discover what God did for them. Then I will know what I can expect Him to do for me. I need to know how others have struggled and emerged victorious. I desire to be assured that the God who helped them is the same God who promises to help me. The more I know of Him, the fewer doubts I have about my circumstances. Instead of being the victim of our doubts, we need to take the initiative and confront them.

HOW SHOULD WE CONFRONT OUR DOUBTS?

We need to face our doubts with a *God-focus* toward life. Identify some of those special qualities about God, such as His great power. No power exists to equal God. Neither man, nor angel, nor demon can defeat God. What may be a major problem for you or me to deal with is a minor matter for God to handle.

God is all-knowing. He knows the exact solution to your problem. He has the perfect wisdom about how you should handle the matter, and He is willing to share that wisdom with you if you ask.

God is present everywhere simultaneously. This means that though you may be separated physically from a person or a situation, He is not. He is there at this very moment and can work in that person's life or situation. When our sons left home for college, it was a difficult transition. There were times when they experienced some special needs and we were not able to be with them physically. On several occasions I hurt deeply inside, longing to sit down with one of our sons and encourage him eye to eye. I wanted to put my arms around him to reassure him that he was not alone. But I couldn't. Too many hundreds of miles separated us. I had to call on the Lord to do it for me, confident that the Lord was right beside our son, counseling, imparting wisdom and strength, and directing his decisions. Now that both our sons are married, I continue my prayer vigil, trusting the ever-present God to meet them where they are.

Another help in dealing with doubts is to *reflect on the past faithfulness of the Lord*. When my wife first had back surgery in 1978, I wasn't sure how to handle the ordeal. She was always the up and vibrant person in our family. When I would come home from the office, she met me with a smile, inquiring how the day went. Whenever I felt discouraged or tired, she lifted my spirits.

But a few years ago, Linda needed to be encouraged, for she was in great pain and faced the trauma of a second surgery. I didn't know what to tell her since I had never been in the hospital as a patient. I had never experienced a surgeon's knife cutting into my body. I had no idea how dangerous the operation might be and was unaware of what to expect when she came out of the operating room and went into recovery.

However, I had a better idea what to expect this time around. I knew the recovery would be painful and probably longer since it was the second time. And since the Lord had been so faithful in helping us through the first hardship, I expected He would be just as faithful this time. Oh, there have been anxious moments, periods of discouragement with the slow recovery. We still don't know the long-range effect of this operation. However, both my wife and I are confident that the Lord will demonstrate His faithfulness to us in many creative ways as we continually trust in Him.

A third approach I've found helpful in handling doubts is to *observe what God has done in the lives of others.* This includes observation of both biblical characters and contemporary characters. For years David ran from the jealousy and rage of King Saul, but in God's time, he became Israel's new king. Joseph spent several years in prison, forgotten by a man he had helped, yet he was never forsaken by God. The Lord delivered him from prison and made it possible for him to become the second in command over the nation of Egypt. Daniel knew what it was like to have his peers plot against him, resulting in a death sentence to the lions' den.

But the next day the king called to him, "Daniel, servant of the living God, has your God, whom you serve continually, been able to rescue you from the lions?" And this was Daniel's reply: "O king, live forever! My God sent his angel, and he shut the mouths of the lions. They have not hurt me, because I was found innocent in his sight. Nor have I ever done any wrong before you, O king" (Daniel 6:20-22). Because Daniel trusted in the Lord and did not doubt, God not only delivered him from certain death, but He also brought Daniel into the number-two position in the nation of Babylon.

It's been helpful for me to observe how the Lord brought order out of chaos in the lives of friends. One friend lost her son through death and her husband through an unwanted divorce. Another lost a son for a period of time to a commune, where he was exposed to many half-truths and remained confused about what he believed for several years. A third lost his business, was forced to sell at a great loss, and then had to learn an entirely new type of business. A fourth was out of work for over a year and spent agonizing weeks battling loss of self-confidence, anxiety over where the next meal would come from, and wondering when God would open a door of opportunity for him. In every one of these cases, the person who spent time in God's waiting room is today enjoying the faithful provision of the Lord as well as intimate fellowship with Him.

When I found that my observation of others' lives was not enough, I took up the slack by focusing on God's promises. I was particularly impressed with certain passages from the book of Isaiah. Many of them are promises directly from God.

"When you pass through the waters, I will be with you; and when you pass through the rivers, they will not sweep over you. When you walk through the fire, you will not be burned; the flames will not set you ablaze. . . . Do not be afraid, for I am with you." (Isaiah 43:2,5)

"Forget the former things; do not dwell on the past. See, I am doing a new thing! Now it springs up; do you not perceive it? I am making a way in the desert and streams in the wasteland." (Isaiah 43:18-19)

"Even to your old age and gray hairs I am he, I am he who will sustain you. I have made you and I will carry you; I will sustain you and I will rescue you." (Isaiah 46:4)

"I say: My purpose will stand, and I will do all that I please. . . . What I have said, that will I bring about; what I have planned, that will I do." (Isaiah 46:10-11)

"This is what the LORD says—your Redeemer, the Holy One of Israel: 'I am the LORD your God, who teaches you what is best for you, who directs you in the way you should go.'" (Isaiah 48:17)

"Because the Sovereign LORD helps me, I will not be disgraced. Therefore have I set my face like flint, and I know I will not be put to shame. He who vindicates me is near." (Isaiah 50:7-8)

"In all their distress he too was distressed." (Isaiah 63:9)

"This is the one I esteem: he who is humble and contrite in spirit, and trembles at my word." (Isaiah 66:2)

Doubting as you wait for the Lord to carry out His purpose can paralyze your faith. That is why the Lord has provided so many promises in His Word. And by its own testimony, the Bible boasts, "Not one of all the LORD's good promises to the house of Israel failed; every one was fulfilled" (Joshua 21:45). "The LORD is faithful to all his promises and loving toward all he has made" (Psalm 145:13).

Dr. V. Raymond Edmond, former president of Wheaton College, said on many occasions, "Never doubt in the dark what God has revealed in the light." Sometimes the storms of life are so dark and dismal that light just doesn't penetrate. From all appearances, hope has vanished. That's when faith must be put into operation. It's the moment to tell the Lord, "Father, I cannot see how any good can come out of this situation. The pain is so great, I can hardly endure it. But You have promised me You are still in control. You have promised that 'all things work together for good.' I accept those promises as facts and thank You that in Your time, something good will result. In Jesus' name, I trust in Your faithfulness. Amen."

Confronting doubts is a major issue to tackle. Dealing with emotions, which can seem like a roller coaster experience, is just as much of a challenge.

4

Dealing with Your Emotions

Waiting upon God can often be emotionally draining. When a person has relatively little control over the outcome of events, he feels like a victim rather than a decision-maker. Everything is happening to him. A sense of helplessness controls him. He feels perplexed because there are questions with no answers and problems with no solutions. He asks himself: "How could this have happened to me?" "Why does God allow it?" "When will it be over?" "What should I do?" "What is God trying to teach me?"

What emotions can one expect to surface during such critical days? As I faced a difficult period in my ministry, my emotions ran the gamut. I had anticipated potential criticism during the first few months of a new ministry, but not in the areas that had been considered and confirmed as strengths. I thought that as long as people criticized my ideas and methods, I had a lot of room for give and take. But when they complained about my preaching and leadership,

I didn't know where to turn. I was so astonished that I didn't know how to respond.

Without question, there were areas in my life and ministry that needed improvement. I welcomed constructive suggestions in both my preaching and leadership. One friend critiqued several messages and then met with me for breakfast and shared some excellent constructive suggestions, for which I was grateful. However, when the complaints took the form of "You're just not a leader," or "I just don't get anything out of your preaching," I faced an unsolvable problem. My emotions included feelings of helplessness, discouragement, grief, confusion, and eventually hopelessness. My major source of encouragement came from the Scriptures, which I investigated carefully, to see how other men dealt with their emotions. The men with whom I most identified were Job, Moses, and Elijah.

JOB'S ENCOUNTER WITH GRIEF

Job was a righteous man, innocent of any wrongdoing. Yet he experienced a grief beyond the understanding of most people. He ached to the very core of his being. Job lost his children through a catastrophic event. Then his wealth and possessions were taken from him overnight, and the health he once enjoyed disappeared, only to be replaced with loathsome boils. This was a new experience for Job. For many years life had treated him well. He was a faithful servant of God, a caring father, a loving husband, and apparently a businessman of impeccable integrity. Despite all of this, Job experienced unprecedented grief.

While in the depths of grief, Job never cursed God, but he did curse the day he was born: "May the day of my birth perish, and the night it was said, 'A boy is born!' That day—may it turn to darkness; may God above not care about it; may no light shine upon it. . . . Why did I not perish at birth, and die as I came from the womb?" (Job 3:3-4,11). To put it mildly, Job was disturbed to the point of despair, which affected him in many ways:

Inability to eat—"Is tasteless food eaten without salt, or is there flavor in the white of an egg? I refuse to touch it; such food makes me ill" (Job 6:6-7).

Fear of both the present and the future—"Only grant me these two things, O God, and then I will not hide from you: Withdraw your hand far from me, and stop frightening me with your terrors" (Job 13:20-21).

A broken heart—"My face is red with weeping, deep shadows ring my eyes. . . . My spirit is broken, my days are cut short, the grave awaits me" (Job 16:16, 17:1).

Loss of hope—"Where then is my hope? Who can see any hope for me? Will it go down to the gates of death? Will we descend together into the dust?" (Job 17:15-16).

Impatience in waiting for God—"Is my complaint directed to man? Why should I not be impatient?" (Job 21:4).

Frustration with unjust accusers—"As surely as God lives, who has denied me justice, the Almighty, who has made me taste bitterness of soul, as long as I have life within me, the breath of God in my nostrils, my lips will not speak wickedness, and my tongue will utter no deceit. I will never admit you are in the right; till I die, I will not deny my integrity" (Job 27:2-5).

Obviously, Job experienced extreme emotional turmoil. He despaired of his very life. Job was not inclined to be ashamed of his emotions. He did not attempt to deny them as though they were sinful in themselves. God gave Job all of his emotions. Though he wallowed for a while in his terrible situation, he emerged as a man who encountered God as few men ever have. Job's despair turned to hope and his complaint to praise. He refused to use his feelings of grief as an opportunity to curse God (Job 2:9-10).

You may feel like Job at this very moment. Everything may seem hopeless to you. But remember that even a man who lost it all, Job, continued to hope in God and was eventually repaid for his faithfulness.

The example of Job became a great encouragement to me when I had my first encounter with grief at the age of twenty-one. It was about twelve midnight and I was studying for an exam at college. One of the guys in the dorm knocked on my door and said, "Rick, you've got an emergency phone call." When I answered I heard my dad's voice at the other end, "Rick, your mother just went home to be with the Lord." His words shot a numbness through my body. I thought to myself, "I must be dreaming. She can't be dead. She's only forty-four years old. No one dies at that age."

The words of Job surfaced from my subconscious and I replied to Dad, "The Lord gave and the Lord has taken away; may the name of the Lord be praised" (Job 1:21). Then I added, "I'll be home as soon as I can." On my way to Lancaster from Philadelphia, I sobbed, prayed, sang hymns, praised the Lord, questioned Him, and anguished in my soul. I kept hoping that somehow I'd awaken from this nightmare, but when I did arise the next morning, reality set in. Mother was gone and would not be coming back until the Lord returns.

For people who spend time in God's waiting room, grief is a common experience—perhaps the loss of something or someone very close. When your spirit has been crushed, you may want to throw in the towel or do something you'll later regret. At such a time, you need to take charge of whatever is within your control and make plans to do something productive while you're waiting. For instance, I have used my own waiting period to write this book. Only recently have I emerged from the longest waiting time of my life, about two years. In the most intense period of waiting, I have invested my time writing this book with the hope that all who read it will be comforted, encouraged, and challenged to make the waiting room experience a productive time rather than wasted time. As I have waited on the Lord, I've placed my confidence in this promise: "The LORD is close to the brokenhearted and saves those who are crushed in spirit" (Psalm 34:18).

If you're not careful, grief can immobilize you. But anger has perhaps even more power to trigger other emotions, attitudes, and actions, if it is not controlled. One man who had great difficulty controlling his temper was Moses.

MOSES' ENCOUNTER WITH ANGER

The Scriptures reveal several times when Moses lost his cool. His first major bout with anger caused Moses to supplant God's plan with his own. He was about forty years of age at the time. Though he had been brought up in Pharaoh's court and educated in all the wisdom of the Egyptians, Moses developed a deep concern for his own people, the Hebrews.

One day as he was visiting the Hebrews, who had been subjected to slave labor, he noticed an Egyptian taskmaster mistreating one of the Hebrew slaves. In anger, Moses attacked the Egyptian and killed him. This of course infuriated the Pharaoh, and so Moses had to leave Egypt and flee for his life. He did not return to Egypt for forty years, and then only under the orders of God.

What was Moses trying to accomplish by killing the Egyptian? Dr. Luke, writer of the book of Acts, offers this insight into Moses' thought process: "Moses thought that his own people would realize that God was using him to rescue them, but they did not" (Acts 7:25). The Lord planned to use Moses for that purpose forty years later, but Moses insisted on achieving the objective according to his own time schedule. Anger encourages a person to take matters into his own hands, thus preempting God's time schedule.

On another occasion, Moses' anger caused him to dishonor God. The Israelites needed water in the desert and demanded that Moses provide it for them. Moses' only recourse was to cry out to God, who instructed him, "Speak to that rock before their eyes and it will pour out its water" (Numbers 20:8). Moses called the people together to provide water for them. As they gathered, Moses shouted to them in anger, "'Listen, you rebels, must we bring you water out of this rock?' Then Moses raised his arm and struck the rock twice with his staff" (20:10-11). By striking the rock in anger instead of speaking to it as God had instructed him, Moses dishonored the Lord, taking credit for what God alone was able to do. That uncontrolled anger cost Moses the opportunity to take Israel into the Promised Land (20:12).

One other fit of anger cost Moses a copy of the Ten Commandments. He had to retrace his steps and start all over again, asking God for a second set of stone tablets: "When Moses approached the camp and saw the calf and the dancing, his anger burned and he threw the tablets out of his hands, breaking them to pieces at the foot of the mountain" (Exodus 32:19). Moses' anger was justified, but his demonstration of anger was not. It's important to distinguish between the two. You may feel very angry inside because someone has taken advantage of you. That person may have hurt you deeply and need to be disciplined by God for his actions. Anger will probably be your natural emotional response for what has happened, but you need to decide how you should express your anger.

NOT ALL ANGER IS SINFUL

Anger in itself is not sinful. The apostle Paul wrote, "'In your anger do not sin': Do not let the sun go down while you are still angry, and do not give the devil a foothold" (Ephesians 4:26-27). It is possible to feel anger without sinning against God. However, this anger must not be prolonged. If it is, the Devil can gain a foothold in the angry person's life and take advantage of him. Anger has the potential to erode your attitude and thinking. You may find yourself rehashing the issue in your mind again and again until you can't stand it anymore. It can tear you apart. Such anger needs to be dealt with quickly.

Jesus directed His anger toward the moneychangers who were treating His Father's house with contempt. He drove them out of the Temple with whips. His anger was righteous and His actions were proper because the religious leaders were making a mockery of God, disregarding the intended purpose of the Temple. They had exchanged the glory due to God for personal profit. We see that Jesus' expression of anger was quick and effective.

The apostle Paul became angry when Peter played the hypocrite. He voiced that anger by rebuking Peter in public (Galatians 2:11-14). However, he and Peter did not break their friendship and relationship. Instead, this encounter strengthened the bond between the two, supporting the kind of wisdom expressed centuries earlier in the book of Proverbs: "Rebuke a wise man and he will love you. . . . Rebuke a discerning man, and he will gain knowledge" (Proverbs 9:8, 19:25).

If an expression of anger hurts you or others, then the demonstration is wrong. If it violates God's standards, it also is wrong. But if a demonstration of anger leads to healing, to helping someone, or to honoring God, then it can be considered a proper and healthy manifestation of anger. Anger can be a good emotion if channeled properly, but it will also be devastating if allowed to go unchecked. In addition to the emotions of grief and anger, another feeling that may stifle spiritual and emotional growth is depression.

ELIJAH'S ENCOUNTER WITH DEPRESSION

Everyone experiences times of discouragement. Many people have first-hand experience with the devastating effects of depression. Some cases are very mild, while others can be paralyzing. Depression has many causes. One factor that can generate this emotional low is a physiological imbalance, such as hypoglycemia. Other seeds of depression are repeatedly sown by successive waves of stress over a long period of time. Repeated failures, loss of a job, financial reversals and many other negative encounters can spawn depression.

For a long time I was under the impression that if a person is walking closely with God, he would never take an emotional plunge into the dark cavern of depression. Experience, however, proved me wrong. My baptism into a depressed state of mind and emotion occurred over a three-month period when I was living in California for the first time. Most of it was brought about by mounting stress over an eighteen-month time frame. It hit me unexpectedly, and I was in no way prepared for the consequences.

During that time of depression, I lost about ten pounds due to lack of appetite (that was the only redeeming factor through the entire episode). I maintained a steady case of "free-floating anxiety"—constantly feeling unnerved and jumpy. I was fearful of anything over which I felt I had no control. I was beginning to feel victimized by many events around me. Despair about the future and lack of joy in the present were a constant inner plague. At times, I wasn't sure I would be able to concentrate enough to prepare the message for the following Sunday.

On top of these feelings, my heart would take off in rapid beats, and nothing I did could stop it. I agreed to see a cardiologist and go through all of the tests, which only proved that my problem was not with my heart but rather with my reaction to various sources of stress. Thanks to the Lord's sustaining grace, I never skipped a Sunday of preaching, a meeting, or a counseling opportunity. I was able to carry out my responsibilities, but my emotional battery was continually discharging. I could really empathize with Elijah, and understood something of what he had gone through.

After the great prophet's thrill of victory on Mount Carmel where he publicly defeated over five hundred prophets of Baal, Elijah encountered the threat of a solitary woman named Jezebel. She put out a contract on his life, and he ran in fear. At this point, Elijah projected two clear-cut evidences of his depressed state of mind.

Elijah's depression caused him so much agony that he asked the Lord to remove him from the earth. As he reflected back on recent events, Elijah cried to God, "I have had enough, LORD. . . . Take my life; I am no better than my ancestors" (1 Kings 19:4). He also developed a warped sense of reality. He actually concluded that he was the last of the faithful prophets. He told the Lord, "I have been very zealous for the LORD God Almighty. The Israelites have rejected your covenant, broken down your altars, and put your prophets to death with the sword. I am the only one left, and now they are trying to kill me too" (1 Kings 19:10).

The Lord furnished three simple solutions for Elijah's depression. First, He provided rest and food for the prophet. Many people who go through such periods in life lose both their ability to sleep and their appetite for food. Elijah was so exhausted that he fell into a deep sleep. That was a gracious provision from God. The Lord also recharged Elijah's spiritual batteries by showing Himself to the prophet—not in the powerful wind, nor in the earthquake, nor in the fire. It was in a gentle whisper that God broke through.

There seems no better way for the Lord to minister to someone who is depressed than in a gentle whisper. When I was down, I did not want the Lord to get my attention by clobbering me over the head with a two-by-four. I wasn't looking for some loud clash of thunder. I needed to experience the gentle touch of God, the gentle whisper of His Word, or a heartrending song.

Elijah also needed to be encouraged in the area of purpose for the future. He was now out of a job. He had successfully fulfilled his responsibility when he challenged the prophets of Baal to a contest. Now the encounter was over. Elijah had emerged victorious. Like others who have achieved great success, the prophet had run out of challenges. To make matters worse, he feared for his life. What could God do for him in this area of need? The Lord encouraged Elijah by giving him a new challenge with specific responsibilities: (1) "Anoint Hazael king over Aram," (2) "anoint Jehu . . . king over Israel," and (3) "anoint Elisha . . . to succeed you as prophet" (1 Kings 19:15-16).

Recently, I was talking with a pastor friend who left his church over a year ago and has yet to find a new ministry. He told me that the most difficult problem he has had to face is his self-confidence. It has been shattered. He has asked himself, "Who would want me as their pastor after all this time?" As he continues to wait on the Lord, he desperately wants to hear what Elijah heard: "Your next assignment will be . . . ." Another pastor friend also waits for a new assignment. For him the waiting period has been over a year. He, too, longs to hear from the Lord, "Here is your next appointment."

Why does God immediately open new opportunities for some people while others wait weeks, which turn into months, and maybe even years? I don't know. But I do know that the opportunity will eventually come when the new challenge will be given and rich blessing will once again flow from the One who is full of compassion.

It's difficult to be depressed and simultaneously have a clear and healthy outlook on life. Usually everything is tainted when viewed through the spectacles of depression. In my own state of depression, I found excellent counsel from a friend who gave me a word of hope. He told me that what I was experiencing was normal for someone under great stress. He further encouraged me by telling me my "down time" would probably not last more than three months and that I could anticipate a much more positive outlook on life in the near future. That gave me a ray of hope. It provided the light at the end of the tunnel. To my joy, his prediction was right on target. As I began to think more in terms of God's blessings rather than my problems, over which I had little control, I formed a more positive attitude and outlook on life.

My friend also encouraged me to maintain a routine and to focus on those areas where I could take greater control over events and attitudes. I worked on gaining control over my time, my finances, and my body (physical exercise and diet). I also got myself better organized in my ministry. Gradually, I felt more in control of my life and less like a victim of negative circumstances.

These suggestions proved to be a tremendous benefit when I was really low emotionally. To feel depressed at times is not uncommon. However, to allow this emotion to control your life to the point that you become ineffective, inefficient, or immobilized is to experience an emotion out of control.

Anyone who finds himself in the throes of depression can find strength and hope by meditating on the words of the psalmist: "Though you have made me see troubles, many and bitter, you will restore my life again; from the depths of the earth you will again bring me up. You will increase my honor and comfort me once again" (Psalm 71:20-21). Now that's hope! It must become a personal expectation. God can be trusted. He knows exactly how you and I feel and is as concerned about our misery as He was about Israel's (Exodus 3:7-9). Take courage. Don't self-destruct by telling yourself how awful everything is. A process that has helped me when things look dark includes the following:

To start, I make a list of all the problems that I perceive in my life. Then I put beside each one an M (much), an S (some), or an N (none). Those problems over which I have much control, some control, or no control need to be identified. Here is a sample of how I have rated some subject areas: people's attitudes toward me (S); lack of exercise (M); people's reactions to my decision (N); lack of sleep (M); people's rejection of my plans (S); too much responsibility, too little time (S); feeling disorganized (M); and shortage of financial resources (S).

Let me focus in on the first three problems. The first two can be turned into specific goals. Why? Because if there is something I can do about a problem, then there's something toward which I can aim. But the third problem must be set aside, placed into the Lord's hands, since nothing can be done to change any problem in that category. So here's how I decided to deal with these first three problems:

1. *People's attitudes toward me (S)*—I will do everything possible to clear up any misunderstanding that some people may have concerning my motives, my purpose, or my methods for doing what I am doing. Some may change their attitude once they understand me better, while others may continue to hold a bad attitude toward me. In that situation, I will turn it over to the Lord.

2. *Lack of exercise (M)*—I can do something about this. I will begin an exercise program including jogging, racquetball, and swimming. I will schedule an exercise session at least three times a week.

3. *People's reactions to my decision (N)*—There are some situations over which I have no control, and this is one of them. I must make my decision on the basis of what is right and not on what is expedient or what will please everyone. Some people will not like my decision. They may feel slighted and become angry, resentful, or even vengeful. I must accept that fact and do what I believe will please God and be best for the situation. I cannot allow people's feelings and reactions to control my decision.

Perhaps going through this kind of an analysis of your problems could help you as you work through the mounting issues that demand your attention. To summarize the process: Identify the amount of control you have over each problem, turn some of them into goals, and place the others into the hands of the Lord.

Emotions are not to be denied. At the same time, they should not take control of your life. Accept how you feel about your present situation, but don't let those feelings control you or encourage you to do something you may be ashamed about later. Be encouraged with these words: "Though you have made me see troubles, many and bitter, you will restore my life again; from the depths of the earth you will again bring me up. You will increase my honor and comfort me once again" (Psalm 71:20-21).

5

Waiting Together
with God

Recently I passed the big fifty mark in my life. I wasn't sure what to expect, but determined that I would not be caught off guard as I was when I hit the big forty a decade ago. That I wasn't prepared for. Oh, I heard a lot of jokes about the fortieth year, how the body begins to fall apart and one's perspective on life begins to take a new twist. But I wasn't ready for the aches and pains, the bulges around the waist, the wrinkles under the eyes, and the fuzziness of sight about to invade my healthy, problem-free body.

The problem first became noticeable when I read my Bible in the morning. I would usually place it in my lap with my legs crossed. But as the days passed, I found myself leaning further back in my chair to focus on the print. At first I blamed the publisher for putting such fine print in the Bible. To my dismay I came to realize that the problem did not lie with the publisher, but rather with me and my eyesight. Everything within fifteen to eighteen inches went out of focus. The worst culprit was the Yellow Pages. I had a hard time walking through them because I couldn't see where I was going.

Perhaps we also experience a spiritual mid-life crisis when our spiritual eyesight begins to get out of focus. We experience problems with questionable solutions, so we look to God. As we seek Him, what we see is not clear. His mode of operation, His answers to our prayers, even His purpose for allowing us to get caught up in a trying situation, all make little sense. At one time we seemed to have all our theology straight. We were able to place God in a nice theological box where He never surprised us or did anything out of the ordinary. Now everything seems to have broken loose. As we try to focus on what God might be doing, we see only distortion. God and everything He is doing is out of focus.

When we were young, we took a lot more chances and may even have found it easier to trust God at that stage of our life, probably because we had so little to lose. When we begin to approach retirement age, with potential health problems and financial set-backs; when our kids are in college and every decision we make has a domino effect; when we begin to question our own abilities and wonder whether we could make a go of it if we lost everything—*then* we are not as prone to take leaps of faith. We begin to think about security more than ever before. We even feel guilty for thinking about our future, like we aren't trusting the Lord.

For years we've believed and told others about God's faithfulness and ability to supply all our needs. But now God gives us the opportunity to validate His faithfulness, and we aren't sure we want the opportunity. Has God changed? Is He different today than He was when we were young and healthy? Has He weakened with age? Is He as able now to provide for us as He was years ago? The prophet Isaiah put it well when he unequivocally declared:

> Do you not know? Have you not heard? The LORD is the everlasting God, the Creator of the ends of the earth. He will not grow tired or weary, and his understanding no one can fathom. He gives strength to the weary and increases the power of the weak. Even youths grow tired and weary, and young men stumble and fall; but those who hope in the LORD will renew their strength. They will soar on wings like eagles; they will run and not grow weary, they will walk and not be faint. (Isaiah 40:28-31)

When you and I wait with the Lord in His waiting room, we do so with a sharper vision concerning who He is and what He is able to do. Consider God's description of Himself: "My thoughts are not your thoughts, neither are your ways my ways. As the heavens are higher than the earth, so are my ways higher than your ways and my thoughts than your thoughts" (Isaiah 55:8-9).

God called out to Israel, to those who were thirsting for spiritual water and hungering for spiritual bread. He said, "Seek the LORD while he may be found; call on him while he is near. Let the wicked forsake his way and the evil man his thoughts" (Isaiah 55:1-2, 6-7).

There is a vivid contrast between how man thinks and how God thinks, between man's ways and God's ways. They seldom interface. This implies that one who is truly seeking the Lord will search for the thoughts and ways of God. As he understands God's thoughts and ways, this individual will forsake his own for the Lord's.

God is unique. He stands apart from men in many ways. Obviously, He differs from man in character, for God is perfect while man is sinful. The Lord is also all-knowing, but man possesses limited knowledge. The Lord excels in power and is the Almighty, while man is powerless in the face of the impossible. Consider other ways in which God uniquely stands apart from man. These differences will provide some insight, enabling you to wait with greater confidence in a God who is still in control.

GOD IS UNIQUE IN HIS THOUGHTS

The prophet Isaiah was speaking for the Lord when he wrote, "My thoughts are not your thoughts" (Isaiah 55:8). The word translated "thoughts" is the Hebrew *mahashaba*. It conveys the concept of planning, devising, or creating new ideas. God's ideas and plans differ drastically at times from what we would plan or think.

For instance, before we moved to Minneapolis back in 1984, our plans were to spend the summer in California with our sons. My wife and I had several speaking engagements on the West Coast and in Colorado, so it made sense to remain on the West Coast until August. However, on June 1, 1984, my wife was involved in a car accident and spent the next three months in bed. All of our summer plans changed. I had to travel to my speaking engagements alone while she stayed home in bed. It wasn't pleasant, but that was how we spent the summer of 1984.

The Bible speaks about how our thoughts may at times differ from God's. Think for a moment about the typical businessman who plans to make an important business deal with a potential customer. Everything seems to be in place. The deal looks to be profitable for both parties. However, after the contract is signed and a few months pass, it becomes obvious that this wasn't a good situation after all. One of the parties wants to back out, but he is legally bound and may end up losing a lot of money in the process. His idea and plans were to make a killing on the opportunity, but that may not be the way God saw it.

The apostle James warns us about being presumptuous in our planning:

> Now listen, you who say, "Today or tomorrow we will go to this or that city, spend a year there, carry on business and make money." Why, you do not even know what will happen tomorrow. What is your life? You are a mist that appears for a little while and then vanishes. Instead, you ought to say, "If it is the Lord's will, we will live and do this or that." As it is, you boast and brag. All such boasting is evil. (James 4:13-16)

There is nothing wrong with planning. But planning without God is mere presumption. As you wait for God to work through that situation in which you find yourself, make plans, but do so by seeking God's will to be done. Ask Him for the necessary discernment as you walk through your difficulty.

SAMSON DID NOT THINK LIKE GOD

An individual who thought he knew what was going on in life was Samson. He was a man of great strength and was feared by his enemies. Time and again he defeated the Philistines singlehandedly. No one could take him down. But he became careless with the special gift of strength God had given him. He presumed that he could use it at any time because he thought that God was always with him, even when he violated His laws.

When his unbelieving girlfriend, Delilah, continued to

nag him with questions about the source of his strength, he finally gave in to her nagging. He told her, "No razor has ever been used on my head because I have been a Nazarite set apart to God since birth. If my head were shaved, my strength would leave me, and I would become as weak as any other man" (Judges 16:17).

Once Delilah identified Samson's source of strength, she informed the Philistines. When they came to get him, Delilah called, "'Samson, the Philistines are upon you!' He awoke from his sleep and thought, 'I'll go out as before and shake myself free.' But he did not know that the LORD had left him" (Judges 16:20). What a sad commentary on this man's thoughts. He presumed everything would be as it had been in the past. However, he was unaware that God had left him in the sense of removing the special strength he once possessed. The result was catastrophic. God removed His hand of blessing from Samson, replacing it with His hand of discipline.

It is not difficult to fall into Samson's kind of thought pattern, even when a person is involved in ministry. An individual serves the Lord in His power and for His honor one year after another. As time passes and God blesses his ministry, job, or life in general, he begins to presume on God's favor, thinking that he deserves everything he is receiving. He expects life to continue as before, thus making important decisions based on faulty assumptions. As he becomes careless and fails to inquire what the Lord wants, he inevitably gets himself and others into great difficulty.

Churches have similar problems. The leadership of a church may have experienced a great outpouring of God's blessing over the years. The congregation reaches out to the hurting, the confused, and the spiritually destitute; sends forth missionaries to many parts of the world; increases its budget, staff, facility, and equipment. This church's prestige may even excel both locally and nationally. It may earn the reputation of "the place to be" on Sunday morning, as well as during the week.

As time passes, the church eases into a "business as usual" mentality, meaning that the people feel capable of handling the church's present affairs as in the past, expecting the same degree of success. Rather than seeking the Lord in a spirit of humility, they send up prayers that are basically requests for God to bless what they've already decided to do, based on their presumptuous human ingenuity and wisdom. Eventually they make some major decisions, convinced that "the Lord is still with us and will bless us as before."

However, these people are not aware that their dependence is no longer on the Lord, but rather on themselves. They mistake the whistles and bells of programming for evidence of God's power and blessing. Like Samson, they have become unaware that God has removed His hand of blessing and is about to bring upon them His unavoidable hand of discipline.

When we presume that the present and the future will follow the identical pattern of the past, we will find ourselves in the same basic dilemma as Samson. We may not have the same health, the same amount of money, the same friends, the same opportunities, or the same success we once had. I've already shared with you how I expected the people in Minneapolis to respond in similar fashion as those in Fresno, California. I expected to be as successful in my preaching and leadership as I had been previously. But God had other plans. He wanted me to learn not to depend on past success, nor to be so self-sufficient. The Lord needed to teach me that my dependence should never be on what I have done previously, but rather on Him in the here and now.

PETER DID NOT THINK LIKE GOD

Even the apostle Peter learned that God's thoughts and his thoughts were not always the same. The Scriptures record the event:

> From that time on Jesus began to explain to his disciples that he must go to Jerusalem and suffer many things at the hands of the elders, chief priests and teachers of the law, and that he must be killed and on the third day be raised to life. Peter took him aside and began to rebuke him. "Never, Lord!" he said. "This shall never happen to you!" Jesus turned and said to Peter, "Get behind me, Satan! You are a stumbling block to me; you do not have in mind the things of God, but the things of men." (Matthew 16:21-23)

Peter was not understanding God's plan. Hence, he was not thinking God's thoughts. His intentions seemed right, but when compared with God's purpose, his thoughts proved to be wrong.

You have probably run across some people who are good people. They love the Lord and keep themselves from a lot of trouble. However, they just don't think the thoughts of God. Their reasoning is from human wisdom. Their decision-making is based primarily on experience or what they've observed others doing. They may be on your church board, in your Sunday school leadership, or on your church staff. They may even be in your own family.

These people think in terms of expediency more than in terms of truth. Their thoughts focus more on what people might say than on what is the right thing to do according to God's truth. They bring their experience from the outside world into the church, and then make decisions about running the church as they would in running a business, a corporation, or some other secular organization.

In what way are a person's thoughts different from God's? The difference can be seen whenever someone is convinced that he knows what is best. If you were to ask a child whether he wanted to consume ice cream, cake, and soda pop before going to bed, he'd probably take you up on the offer because he sees no harm in filling his body with sugar before going to sleep. He is in no position to determine what is best for him. He will make his decision based on what he wants, not on what is best.

Adults follow a similar pattern when they see opportunities and material things that appeal to their senses and egos. They usually don't ask questions like, "Is this really best for me?" Unless they are finely tuned to God's guidance in their lives, the decision will be based on what they want or what they've convinced themselves is best.

Another mode of thinking that differs from God's is when one believes that he is in control of life. He assumes that most of life centers around his ability to control people and circumstances. If he cannot control at first, he may go into a manipulation mode to bring others around to his way of thinking. Then in His wisdom, God brings into that individual's life someone who refuses to be manipulated or coerced. Such a person may be a boss, a subordinate, a husband or wife, or even one's own child. As the situation gets out of control, the individual is forced to call on the Lord.

A person is thinking quite differently from God whenever he believes that he can run his life as he desires without suffering the consequences of his actions. In spite of all the evidence of others who have split their families, hurt their friends, and messed up their own lives because of their wrong thinking, some individuals feel that somehow they are different. They justify their attitudes and actions, believing in some way that God buys into their game of mental gymnastics. Eventually they suffer the consequences of their decisions, but they wonder how God could allow such terrible consequences to be part of life.

Whenever someone thinks he is above the problems of normal humanity, his thoughts are in great contrast to the thoughts of God. It's the other guy who has problems with his marriage or kids, loses his job, or suffers from a terminal disease. Other people suffer emotional breakdowns, burnout, tragedy, drunkenness, drug abuse, child abuse, wife abuse, and other such difficulties. Then one day he awakens to the fact that it has happened to him. He is the statistic, the victim, or the instigator. His thoughts about immunity to life's problems are suddenly shattered into reality.

Joseph did not think he would have to spend an extra two years in a prison cell, but because the man he had helped forgot him, Joseph suffered another two years (Genesis 40:12-41:14). Abraham did not think it would take twenty-five years before he would experience the fulfillment of God's promised son, but that's how long it took from the promise to the reality (Genesis 15:4, 21:1-5).

You may be wanting something to happen so badly that you can hardly wait until it occurs. But God may have an entirely different timetable. He does not think like you and me when it comes to time. Peter commented about God's perspective of time when he wrote, "Do not forget this one thing, dear friends: With the Lord a day is like a thousand years, and a thousand years are like a day" (2 Peter 3:8).

What personal thoughts have you discovered to be different from God's (for example, places you expected to live, jobs you expected to have, and events you expected to take place that never came to pass)? God is unique in His thoughts. But He is also unique in His ways, for He says, "Neither are your ways my ways" (Isaiah 55:8).

Sometimes it seems to us as though God is going the wrong direction. The Hebrew word translated "way" means a path worn by constant walking. God's paths may differ drastically from ours. At certain times they make very little sense. The disciples failed to see any significance in the Cross until after the Resurrection. Consider some other paths of the Lord that would not have been chosen by His servants.

GOD TOOK ISRAEL ON AN EXTENDED JOURNEY

God led the people of Israel through a detour as they traveled across the desert toward the Promised Land. Why? The answer is given in the book of Exodus: "When Pharaoh let the people go, God did not lead them on the road through the Philistine country, though that was shorter. For God said, 'If they face war, they might change their minds and return to Egypt.' So God led the people around by the desert road toward the Red Sea. The Israelites went up out of Egypt armed for battle" (Exodus 13:17-18).

The shortest distance between two points may be a straight line, but God does not always want us to travel the shortest distance. We are by nature impatient people. We would like to see God accomplish what needs to be done in the shortest amount of time possible, especially if we are sitting in a waiting room. Our first response may be, "Lord, let's get this problem settled. Let's get it over with so that I can move on with my life." That is often our desire, but it is not usually His way.

We may not know why He takes us through the desert or the barren places, where we see very little life. Everything seems to be dry. We become tired, thirsty, weary. We look for the refreshing oasis, but see only the mirage. God has His reasons for the extended journey, reasons that He may reveal to us at a later time. Then again, we may never know this side of eternity why we experienced the delay.

GOD REDIRECTED PAUL'S PATH

Consider another situation, this time in the life of Paul. He desired to preach the gospel in places where it was never preached. He made plans to preach in Asia. It was a logical decision to move into that territory. After all, the people needed the gospel as much in Asia as anywhere else. But notice what happened when he tried to go: "Paul and his companions traveled throughout the region of Phrygia and Galatia, having been kept by the Holy Spirit from preaching the word in the province of Asia" (Acts 16:6).

We do not know *why* the Holy Spirit prevented the message from penetrating Asia at that time, or even *how* He prevented their travel to Asia. We only know that Paul and his companions were not able to carry out their plans. When some believers are in a similar situation, they blame the Devil or another person. They fail to understand that, for His own reasons, God may keep us from achieving what may be a good idea, but with the wrong timing or in the wrong place.

Paul ran into a similar situation later in his travels: "When they came to the border of Mysia, they tried to enter Bithynia, but the Spirit of Jesus would not allow them to" (Acts 16:7). Again, the prevention came from God, not from an enemy. The desire and intention of preaching the gospel was good, but that place at that time did not fit God's way. So the Lord closed the door. Paul and his colleagues eventually went west to Macedonia where God had planned for them to go all along (Acts 16:8-10). The Lord honored their desire to preach the gospel, but directed them to a different location.

How does this even affect us today? Perhaps you wanted to live in a certain location and made plans to move in that direction, but your path was blocked by some unforeseen circumstance. You may have tried another direction, but your path was blocked again. Before you blame the circumstances or say, "This must be of the Devil," take another look at the possibility of God's intervention. He may be protecting you from an unknown trap or problem in those other locations. He may be preparing you for a very fruitful life somewhere else.

When I graduated from seminary in 1964, I had planned to become a Christian education director. I had my eyes on California, but told the Lord that I was willing to go wherever He wanted to send me. A pastor from Santa Ana, California, came to the seminary to interview several students for a Christian education position in his church. The chemistry was strong between the pastor and me, so my wife and I thought that a move to California was inevitable. But a letter one week later changed all of that. The pastor informed us that another man had been chosen for that position. Of course we were greatly disappointed, but we told the Lord that we meant what we said earlier about going where He wanted us to go.

Our commitment took us to Minneapolis, Minnesota, for three years, then on to Winnipeg, Canada, for almost five years, and eventually out to Fresno, California, where we spent thirteen years building a ministry. After the Fresno experience, we traveled back to Minneapolis for a few more years. And we now have a ministry within a few miles of Santa Ana, California, where the door had been closed twenty-three years earlier. I call that a "full cycle."

If I had initially gone to the church in Santa Ana, my

life and the life of others would have been quite different. I probably would not have become part of the Evangelical Free Church, which would have been a great loss. Most likely I would not have had the opportunity to write, for that ministry opened for me through a contact I had while living in Fresno, California. Furthermore, the church in Fresno would have had a very different history. I think of all the friends Linda and I would never have met. Our son Steven would not have met his wife Nancy. It is doubtful that either of our sons would be preparing for ministry today because their decision grew out of the influence of Tim Smith, their youth director in Fresno.

In fact, thinking about the possible ramifications of directions taken in life reminds me of the movie the networks run every Christmas season, *It's a Wonderful Life,* where Jimmy Stewart has an encounter with an angel. The celestial visitor takes Jimmy Stewart on a tour of life as it would have been if he had never been born. Quite an interesting angle.

God is unique in His thoughts and His ways. He is also unique in His perspective on life. The Lord looks more at the reality than at the appearance of reality.

GOD IS UNIQUE IN HIS PERSPECTIVE

There was a time in the history of Israel when God told Samuel to anoint a new king, since King Saul had been unfaithful to Him. As Samuel went to the house of Jesse, he asked that all of Jesse's sons be brought before him so that he could anoint one of them as king. The first son, Eliab, was brought to Samuel. As soon as Samuel saw Eliab he thought, "Surely the LORD's anointed stands here before the LORD" (1 Samuel 16:6). It made sense. He looked like a king. He walked like a king. In every way he seemed to be the perfect candidate. Only one problem: He was not God's anointed. To Samuel he appeared to be the likely candidate, but to God he was not.

In what ways do man's perceptions differ from God's? One contrast is what I call the *appearance focus*. We have the tendency to look at what appears attractive, opportune, exciting, and trustworthy. The passage continues, "But the LORD said to Samuel, 'Do not consider his appearance or his height, for I have rejected him. The LORD does not look at the things man looks at. Man looks at the outward appearance, but the LORD looks at the heart'" (1 Samuel 16:7). We seek what looks good. We enjoy the flash, the excitement, the super-hero type. We desire to be head and shoulders above everyone else in our choices. But God zeros in on the heart. He looks for what is on the inside.

How often are people fooled when they go to buy a used car? They look at the new paint job, the engine that has just been steam cleaned, and the new tires, remarking, "This is it. It's in perfect condition. Just look at how clean it is." But after a few weeks they sadly discover that they've just bought a lemon. The outside looked great, but the inside was another story.

Many people choose their mate on the basis of physical attraction. A woman may search for the tall, dark, and handsome male, while the man goes for the shapely, attractive female. As the years pass, so does the shape, the hair, and the attraction. The tight, smooth skin is replaced by wrinkles. The chest sinks slowly into the waistline and the fine curves into bulging hips. The ability to do what one wants eventually gives way to doing what one can. If many of our decisions are based primarily on what looks good, we could be in for a shocking disappointment later in life.

Another contrast between God's perspective and ours is the *precedent focus*. Samuel thought that Eliab would make a good king. Why? One can only conjecture, but precedent may have played a role in Samuel's thinking. There may have been several similarities between Eliab and King Saul. Being the oldest son, it would have made sense for Eliab to be God's anointed, but there may also have been a resemblance between Eliab and Saul in manner or appearance.

A third difference in perspective is the *circumstance focus*. We observe the circumstances and conclude, "This must be the Lord's will because everything is falling so well into place." I had such an encounter about twenty years ago. The senior pastor under whom I had worked as a Christian education director was leaving for another church. I also was aware that the Lord was tugging at my own life to head in another direction. I just wasn't certain where that would be, though the thought of going back to school for another graduate degree had passed through my mind.

One Sunday afternoon, my wife and I were sitting by one of the beautiful lakes in the city where a man, his wife, and child were about to enter a canoe, tied to a tree within a few feet of us. I immediately recognized the man as one of the professors at the University in the Communications Department. I walked over to help him get his canoe untied and into the water. As we talked, I shared with him my plans to enter the University and work on a graduate program in the area of communications. He was delighted to hear my idea and made an appointment with me for the next day. The professor showed me around the department, introduced me to other professors, gave me some brochures on the purpose and direction of the department, and encouraged me to follow through with my plans.

Everything fell into place so perfectly. Even the chance meeting at the lake could easily have been interpreted as ordained of God. However, there was something deep inside that continued to give me unrest. It was as though I was fighting something. I shared my situation with Dr.

Haddon Robinson, president of Denver Seminary. He asked me whether I had ever considered being a pastor. I told him that the thought had crossed my mind many times, but that I had been able to successfully dispel the notion. I felt that pastoring a church would be one of the last choices I would want to make.

However, the more we talked, the more I realized I was wrestling with God, fearful that He might one day take me up on the commitment I had made at the age of twelve, to do whatever He wanted me to do. I soon became convinced that this encounter with my former professor was not an accident, but rather directed by the Spirit of God, who opened my eyes to see how I had been fighting against what He had wanted me to do. In spite of the circumstantial evidence at the lake, the Lord was not leading me to further my education in communications.

A fourth perspective is the *money focus,* where decisions are based on which job pays the most rather than on which direction the Lord may be leading. God may not always want us to accept the position that will give us the greatest financial return. Too many other values need to be considered apart from the financial gain.

For others the primary contrast between their perspective and God's is the *comfort focus.* Whatever happens to be the most comfortable and the least likely to demand change becomes the key issue. The Lord may open an excellent opportunity for these people to stretch their faith, but because that would remove them from their comfort zone and take away their security blanket, they turn down the option.

God virtually had to push the early Christians out of Jerusalem in order to penetrate the world with the gospel because they had become very comfortable within the city. The Lord told His disciples to go into all the world with the gospel, but they stopped at the city gates. Therefore, He allowed persecution to drive them out of the city and into Judea, Samaria, and the uttermost parts of the earth. Perhaps God may have to do the same thing to get believers today to move in His direction by refocusing their eyes.

One further contrast of perspective can be seen in the *problem focus.* Some people are so problem-oriented they can never see the potential in the problem. Everything looks like doom and gloom. They center their attention on everything that is going wrong and fail to see all of the aspects of life that are going right. God is a realist. He sees the problems, but He also knows the solutions to those problems. He wants us to gain His perspective on all of those issues that we call problems and impossibilities. With God, nothing is impossible, so our perspective must become positive rather than negative.

God is unique in His thoughts, His ways, and His perspective. Therefore, when you wait, be sure to wait with Him. Try to think as He thinks and to see as He sees. And be encouraged by His message to you when He says, "I am the LORD your God, who teaches you what is best for you, who directs you in the way you should go" (Isaiah 48:17).

As you meditate on this promise, which cannot fail, why not turn it into prayer and respond with this request: "Dear Father, since You know what is best for me, please make it known to me so that I might do it. Because You know the direction I should go, You have my complete permission and full cooperation to take me in that direction. I promise to follow You wherever that leads."

This was my prayer as I entered God's waiting room. Today this prayer has been answered. He has satisfied my desires far beyond my imagination. I've learned through waiting with God that He can be trusted with everything I have and with what I may have or may be in the future.

6

A Support System

It is always difficult to wait for the unknown. Whether you are in a hospital, waiting for news about the family member you just brought into the emergency room, or whether you are waiting to hear if you got the job for which you recently interviewed, the unknown can drive you up the wall. When you wait alone, that adds misery to anxiety.

God never intended for us to wait by ourselves. He has provided support systems that can be a tremendous benefit to help lessen the anxiety that often builds during those times of silence. Besides the support of God's Word and His Holy Spirit, the Lord has provided human support systems, including family, friends, and the Church.

THE FAMILY AS A SUPPORT SYSTEM

One observation I've made over the years is the emphasis on the close-knit families of biblical times. They had their squabbles and fights, but even in the midst of such common problems, the family became a tremendous support basis for any person in trouble. For instance, consider Joseph's family. Though they were not much of a support for him as he went through his waiting room experience, he became a great support to them when they were in trouble. He was convinced that God was the One who had sent him to Egypt in order to provide for the future needs of his family.

When a famine arose in the land, Jacob sent his sons to Egypt to buy grain. When the sons arrived and appeared before Joseph, they were not aware that they were speaking to the brother they had sold to a passing caravan years before. When Joseph revealed his identity to them, they were terrified, convinced that their lives were in danger. But because of Joseph's own conviction that God allowed him to experience troubles for the good of his family's future, he responded to his brothers in a generous and unusual fashion:

> "Do not be distressed and do not be angry with your-selves for selling me here, because it was to save lives that God sent me ahead of you. For two years now there has been famine in the land, and for the next five years there will not be plowing and reaping. But God sent me ahead of you to preserve for you a remnant on earth and to save your lives by a great deliverance. So then, it was not you who sent me here, but God." (Genesis 45:5-8)

The record of Joseph's generosity continues: "So Joseph settled his father and his brothers in Egypt and gave them property in the best part of the land, the district of Rameses, as Pharaoh directed. Joseph also provided his father and his brothers and all his father's household with food, according to the number of their children" (Genesis 47:11-12).

The Lord also provided a support system for Moses. He was called by God to go into the land of Egypt and rescue the Israelites. God promised that He would go with Moses, but out of fear and in need of a human companion, Moses was reluctant to proceed by himself. Without human support, Moses would have felt isolated. Therefore, God offered him the support of his brother. The Lord inquired:

> "What about your brother, Aaron the Levite? I know he can speak well. He is already on his way to meet you, and his heart will be glad when he sees you. You shall speak to him and put words in his mouth; I will help both of you speak and will teach you what to do. He will speak to the people for you, and it will be as if he were your mouth and as if you were God to him." (Exodus 4:14-15)

It's interesting when the Lord places two brothers in a home. Often they are a contrast of personality, interest, and ability. Esau and Jacob were opposites. Esau was a hunter, loving the outdoors, while Jacob, a manipulator, accomplished things through shrewd dealings.

Our sons are also opposites. Their looks, interests, and personalities are quite different, though both plan to serve the Lord professionally. One has greater athletic interests, while the other, who physically could have been either a wrestler or a football player, enjoys music. One is more of a romantic and right-brain oriented (holistic thinking, less involved with detail, feeling-oriented), while the other is more left-brain oriented (logical, sequential, analytical).

Moses and Aaron fit the mold of opposites as well. Aaron was outgoing, possessing excellent communication skills, while Moses was more action-focused and not as well-developed in communication. When God told him to return to Egypt for the unprecedented assignment of delivering several million people from slavery, he instantly replied, "Oh Lord, I have never been eloquent, neither in the past nor since you have spoken to your servant. I am slow of speech and tongue" (Exodus 4:10).

Not strong enough in his faith to accept God's challenge by himself, Moses pleaded for a helper. God acquiesced to Moses' requests by sending his brother Aaron to him. The Lord responded, "I know he can speak well. . . . I will help both of you speak and will teach you what to do. He will speak to the people for you, and it will be as if he were your mouth" (Exodus 4:14-16). So Aaron supported Moses throughout the next forty years of ministry.

It is important to note that this provision was not God's first choice and that in the long run, it was not in Moses' best interest. On two occasions, Aaron became a stumbling block to Moses, causing him a great amount of stress and grief. When Moses was up on the mountain, receiving the Ten Commandments from God, Aaron was at the foot of the mountain, making a golden calf and leading the people into idolatry (Exodus 32). On another occasion, Aaron joined his sister, Miriam, and together they challenged Moses' authority (Numbers 12).

Sometimes those in our own family can become a stumbling block between ourselves and the will of the Lord. At other times they become a wonderful support system. After the exodus from the land of Pharaoh, God continued to give Moses support. This time He used Moses' father-in-law, Jethro, who taught Moses how to organize for greater efficiency and effectiveness (Exodus 18).

Perhaps the Lord is directing you to provide in some way for members of your own family. An aging parent may need your physical or financial support. The apostle Paul cautioned young Timothy, "If anyone does not provide for his relatives, and especially for his immediate family, he has denied the faith and is worse than an unbeliever" (1 Timothy 5:8).

Or maybe your family needs your emotional support. A parent who is never satisfied with his child's athletic, academic, musical, or social accomplishments, plants seeds of emotional turmoil in that child's life. On the other hand, a parent may need emotional support from his or her children. A parent needs to hear his children express appreciation, love, and affirmation of worth. All parents need to hear a "thank you" or "I love you" from the lips and hearts of their children.

Many parents feel they've failed to rear their children properly, especially when a child gets into trouble or becomes rebellious. These parents feel guilty and may spend long hours pondering the past: "What did I do wrong? What should I have done differently?" This is why children need to affirm their parents.

Spiritual support within the family is also essential. God has chosen the father to be the spiritual head of the family. Following the example of Job, who interceded for his children daily, fathers need to support their children spiritually. In concert with the father, the mother in the family should also play a major role in giving spiritual support to their children. Unless the mother is working outside the home, she will spend more time with her children than her husband is able to. Therefore, she has a greater opportunity to impact her children spiritually during the day. In some cases, it's the children who become God's instrument to introduce their parents to Jesus Christ and provide spiritual support. God uses family members to be a physical, emotional, and spiritual support system when someone is in God's waiting room. I found this to be true during my own waiting room experience.

My family became an ideal means of support when I returned to Pennsylvania for about ten days, soon after resigning from my pastoral position. My folks gave me breathing room within the house. I had my own space, no time pressures, and no demands placed on me. The reprieve gave me time to be with the Lord in prayer and in His Word; to jog each day for physical exercise; and to think, reflect and begin to plan for the future.

At the same time, the members of my family were available when I wanted to talk with them about my situation. They did not initiate conversation, but served as a sounding board when I was ready to discuss the issues I was grappling with. While I visited family in Pennsylvania, my wife and sons were in the Midwest, upholding me in prayer. As I spent those days with my folks, I recognized how blessed I was to have such a supportive family. They made the waiting room experience bearable. My family was most encouraging, but my support system reached beyond family, extending to my friends.

FRIENDS AS A SUPPORT SYSTEM

"A man of many companions may come to ruin, but there is a friend who sticks closer than a brother" (Proverbs 18:24). When you are going through a time of deep hurt, despair, or emotional agony, you need a friend. You may be surrounded by a lot of people, but sometimes the multitude becomes part of the stress. You don't need a lot of people surrounding you, but you do need a friend.

In his book *Stress and the Bottom Line*, Dr. E. M. Gherman agrees with the principle that good friends are good medicine:

People who are functioning members of their community, are "socially healthy," and also tend to have a higher degree of psychological health and physical well-being. Those people who have developed a source of social support, who have close friendships, strong family ties, and warm relationships with neighbors and fellow-workers, generally deal more effectively with stressful events than those who are socially isolated.

According to the Bible, friends play a major role in times of trouble: "A friend loves at all times, and a brother is born for adversity" (Proverbs 17:17). That's when you need a friend: when your whole world is falling apart. A true friend will tell you what you need to hear, which is not always what you want to hear. He will level with you because he loves you. Your friend may even be willing to jeopardize your friendship to help you. What he says may not soften the blow or lessen the hurt that results from hearing the truth, but his willingness to address the issue gives evidence that he cares enough to risk the friendship. Like a skilled surgeon, he may cause short-term pain for the sake of long-term health.

Solomon showed great wisdom when he wrote, "Better is open rebuke than hidden love. Wounds from a friend can be trusted, but an enemy multiplies kisses" (Proverbs 27:5-6). The great poet and statesman again stated well the benefits of binding friendships:

> Two are better than one, because they have a good return for their work: If one falls down, his friend can help him up. But pity the man who falls and has no one to help him up! Also, if two lie down together, they will keep warm. But how can one keep

warm alone? Though one may be overpowered, two can defend themselves. A cord of three strands is not quickly broken. (Ecclesiastes 4:9-12)

The benefits include (1) greater profit and productivity in working together, (2) help when one falls down, (3) warmth, (4) defense, and (5) unity.

What type of friend is available to meet you on such an intimate level? In their book *Friends and Friendship*, Jerry and Mary White identify three levels of friends. The first level includes *casual friends*, consisting of people seen regularly in the normal course of living. We know them by their first names and occasionally initiate social contact with them. The second level is *close friends*. This may include coworkers, neighbors, associate friendships we've developed while serving in the church, relatives, and mentors (those who contribute significantly to life in a teaching or guiding way). The third level includes *intimate friends*. This is the inner-circle group. They are the few people with whom we pour out our souls and share our deepest feelings and aspirations. For some people this group may number half a dozen, while for others it may be only one or two.

If you were to evaluate your own support system of friends, who would you include in these categories? Who are your intimate, close, and casual friends? Are you building a support base of friends? Have you been a friend in support of someone going through great difficulty? While I waited for God's next chapter in my life, I so appreciated the way my family supported me. I also received tremendous encouragement from friends on all three levels. In fact, I discovered friends I did not even know I had. Some of the casual friends became intimate, while a few, whom I considered intimate, faded into the sunset.

My friends supported me with prayer, letters, breakfasts, lunches, dinners, social get-togethers, humor, words of encouragement, sharing their homes, cabins, and condos for extended periods of time, and even sharing financial and material gifts. We laughed, talked, cried, prayed, and worked together. I had never experienced so much love as I did during the nine months of waiting and transitioning into the next phase of life and ministry. One of the evidences of that support can be seen in the number of visitors we've had in our home from January to April 1987. My wife and I counted somewhere in the vicinity of fifty guests from Minneapolis plus friends from Fresno, who either stayed in our home, visited our church, or both. They were part of that close and intimate support group during my waiting room experience.

THE CHURCH AS A SUPPORT SYSTEM

The third source for support comes from the Church at large. Jesus was talking to the Church in its embryonic stage when He told His disciples, "A new command I give you: Love one another. As I have loved you, so you must love one another. By this all men will know that you are my disciples, if you love one another" (John 13:34-35).

Jesus knew that these men who had been with Him for three years would need much support. Even when He sent them on various missions, Jesus put them in pairs so that they would have the support of one another. That's why the disciples are so often mentioned in twos: "These are the names of the twelve apostles: first, Simon (who is called Peter) and his brother Andrew; James son of Zebedee, and his brother John; Philip and Bartholomew; Thomas and Matthew the tax collector; James son of Alphaeus, and Thaddaeus; Simon the Zealot and Judas Iscariot, who betrayed him" (Matthew 10:2-4).

After the Church experienced its birth on the day of Pentecost, the need for support of individual members became increasingly critical due to the rapid growth of the Church, as well as the resulting persecution. Luke records the historical account:

> All the believers were one in heart and mind. No one claimed that any of his possessions was his own, but they shared everything they had. With great power the apostles continued to testify to the resurrection of the Lord Jesus, and much grace was upon them all. There were no needy persons among them. For from time to time those who owned lands or houses sold them, brought the money from the sales and put it at the apostles' feet, and it was distributed to anyone as he had need. (Acts 4:32-35)

Does this kind of support occur today? I've seen it time and again. A pastor friend, presently in God's waiting room, is looking for the Lord's next place of ministry. He and his wife have depleted their salary and their savings. Each day has brought new insights into God's ability to provide for their needs. The Lord has provided financial help through various members of a former church, as well as from people who attend other churches. Some churches are as active today as the New Testament Church in caring for their own.

In every one of the churches I've served, the members have provided for one another's financial, emotional, material, and spiritual needs. Whenever a family had a vital need it couldn't meet, other individuals within God's family identified the problem, promoted the opportunity to give support, and followed through with the help. That's what the Body of Christ is all about when it is functioning properly.

In similar fashion, our former church in Minneapolis took care of Linda and me as we went through the transition of waiting for God's next ministry for us. They graciously provided for us in a financial way until we began our new ministry. This helped us not to panic or make a hasty decision to take the first opportunity that came our way. We had time to think, to counsel with friends, and to pray about where the Lord was leading us. I regret to say that some of my colleagues have not been so fortunate.

The early Church took care of its members' physical and financial needs. But it also provided for their spiritual and emotional deficiencies. Paul encouraged, "Brothers, if someone is caught in a sin, you who are spiritual should restore him gently. But watch yourself, or you also may be tempted. Carry each other's burdens, and in this way you will fulfill the law of Christ" (Galatians 6:1-2).

The ministry of restoration no longer exists in many churches. They tend to swing on the proverbial pendulum. In some cases, restoration is replaced with license. People live outside of God's moral and ethical laws without ever being confronted about the issue. So the need for restoration does not surface because there has never been any confrontation, admission of wrongdoing, or repentance. Because fellowship within the church was never lost, there seems to be no need for restoration.

On the other end of the pendulum, when some churches discover a moral or ethical problem in one of their members, they confront that person and then discipline him by disassociating themselves, leaving no opportunity for restoration. In his book *Beyond Forgiveness: The Healing Touch of Church Discipline*, Don Baker tells of a situation in one of his former churches, where they went through the process of restoration and salvaged a man's ministry in the process. After the offender's confession, repentance, nine months of counseling, and submission to the authority and discipline of the church for over two years, restoration occurred. Baker describes the long but profitable ordeal with this conclusion: "We concluded twenty-six of the most difficult and yet most instructive months in the life of our church family. Months of pain and perfecting. Months devoted to salvaging a worthy servant and restoring him to productive ministry."

He continues: "As Martha and I went home that night, the weariness was good, and the need for approval was only slight. We didn't ask whether or not we had done the right thing or said the right thing. We simply relaxed—relaxed with the realization that maybe—just maybe—we had finally done it right. We forgave a fallen brother. But we didn't stop there. Cooperating with God, we moved beyond forgiveness, restoring a sinning saint to a life of meaning and ministry."

One further area of support from the local church is found in the area of personal development of skills and gifts. Paul told his young associate Titus, "Teach the older women to be reverent in the way they live, not to be slanderers or addicted to much wine, but to teach what is good. Then they can train the younger women to love their husbands and children, to be self-controlled and pure, to be busy at home, to be kind, and to be subject to their husbands, so that no one will malign the word of God" (Titus 2:3-5).

Here is an example of an older woman teaching a younger woman the basics of being a wife and mother. The same could be said of an older man teaching a younger man how to be a husband and father. Where can young men and women look today for their role models? Many of them have only their own homes as a context from which to draw, which leaves some in a desperate situation because they do not come from healthy family models. Churches are providing a wonderful support system in this very area. A former church in which my wife and I ministered developed a "Mothers and Others" ministry, where young mothers had the opportunity to come to a support group of older women and learn the basics of being a good wife and mother.

Whether the need is financial and material support, spiritual and emotional support, or personal training on how to be a good husband/father or a good wife/mother, the local church should become that resource. When it functions on this level, the church fulfills the biblical mandate: "Encourage one another and build each other up, just as in fact you are doing. . . . And we urge you, brothers, warn those who are idle, encourage the timid, help the weak, be patient with everyone" (1 Thessalonians 5:11,14).

You may be thinking, "I can't argue with the idea, but I don't feel right asking for help. I believe that God wants me to take care of myself and not be dependent on other people." Such an attitude may indicate a heart of pride, which God resists (James 4:6). Jesus was not too proud to receive help from a handful of women who, out of their personal finances, supported Him and the disciples (Luke 8:1-3). Nor was Paul too proud to accept the help of other believers when he was in need. He wrote to his supporters, "It was good of you to share in my troubles. Moreover, as you Philippians know, in the early days of your acquaintance with the gospel, when I set out from Macedonia, not one church shared with me in the matter of giving and receiving, except you only; for even when I was in Thessalonica, you sent me aid again and again when I was in need" (Philippians 4:14-16).

There was a time in my own life when I didn't think I needed either family, friends, or the church as a support group. I could manage most of my problems on my own. Many testified, to my embarrassment, "Rick doesn't seem to need people. He is so self-sufficient." But the time arrived when I could no longer depend upon my wisdom, experience, or any other inherent resource to deal with some of the problems I faced.

During my last year of ministry in Fresno, which occurred in 1984, I felt an extreme amount of stress, even though everything was going well at the church. On the surface things couldn't be better. But deep within, I knew I had run out of challenges. I recognized that I was in a maintenance mode. The gleam had disappeared from my eyes and I felt that I was just marking time.

On top of my concern about purpose in ministry, I became anxious about a possible relocation. "How will I be able to support my family if I make a move? With two sons in college, I will need no less than what both Linda and I are bringing home," or so I thought. I anxiously wondered, "Where will I go? What will I do?"

Although I realized my need for counsel, I didn't know who I could trust with such questions. I threw out a couple of test balloons to some close friends without revealing the true intent of my inquiry. Most of them picked up on the area of emotional stress and were willing to back me one hundred percent, but did not perceive where I was going with the deeper questions about my future. I kept too many of my real feelings to myself.

This brought me to the conclusion that I would have to be more transparent and vulnerable. I'd have to share my intention of leaving. I finally decided to convey my innermost thoughts to a good friend, who had also been a pastor for many years. He was the visitation pastor of our staff. I had full confidence that he would remain objective and be able to offer sound advice, for I knew that he had ministered in numerous churches throughout his career and had to make a similar decision each time.

As I exposed my questions, apprehensions, and fears, Bill asked me a number of questions for clarification, and then he encouraged me to pursue what I thought God was directing me to do. That incident marked a significant change in my perception of friendships. It helped me to realize the importance of having friends.

Also, I drew upon the expertise of three other friends: a psychologist, an opthamologist, and a pharmacist. Allan, Don, and Monte became a great help in teaching me how to handle stressful situations and how to avoid unnecessary stress. Added to this list were two longstanding friends, Dan and Paul, who were always available as the need arose. Waiting on the Lord with friends can make the wait bearable. You have the opportunity to either seek support as you wait or to give support to your friend if he is also waiting on the Lord.

7

The Counsel of His Word

Some people follow instructions with great precision. Others, like myself, will go to great lengths to ignore any written directions and attack a problem with the zeal of a Don Quixote, often with similar results. I've needed to remind myself more than once to go back to the blueprints and proceed accordingly.

Unfortunately, many people approach life in the same manner. In spite of God's written instructions and magnificent blueprint for a fulfilled life, our tendency is to do our own thing. Then when all else fails, we reluctantly read the instructions: the Word of God. The psalmist testified to his use of God's Word as he waited, declaring, "I rise before dawn and cry for help; I have put my hope in your word. My eyes stay open through the watches of the night, that I may meditate on your promises" (Psalm 119:147-148).

What better way to spend time in God's waiting room than to search the Scriptures daily, find His encouragement and directions, and then proceed throughout the day in the power and wisdom of the Holy Spirit! I have personally spent many hours reading the Bible from cover to cover just to acquaint myself with its vast resource of wisdom. I've read the Scriptures when I was discouraged and found my spirit lifted with a new optimism. I was confused and discovered clarity of direction, anxious and experienced calmness, intimidated and became confident once again. The Bible is capable of transforming a life because its very origin is divine. It is a lamp for our feet and a light for our path (Psalm 119:105). Since we are often in the dark about what God is doing, it's imperative to turn to Scripture for enlightenment.

Paul declared his high view of Scripture when he wrote, "All Scripture is God-breathed and is useful for teaching, rebuking, correcting and training in righteousness, so that the man of God may be thoroughly equipped for every good work" (2 Timothy 3:16-17). This passage presents several observations worth investigating.

ALL SCRIPTURE IS GOD-BREATHED

The first emphasis from 2 Timothy 3:16-17 indicates that the totality of Scripture is divinely inspired. Whether one reads the historical books (Genesis, Exodus, Leviticus, the Gospels, Acts, etc.), the poetic books (Psalms, Proverbs, Ecclesiastes, Song of Solomon, etc.), the prophetic books (Isaiah, Jeremiah, Daniel, Joel, Amos, etc.), or the didactic books (the Epistles of Paul, Peter, and John, and the General Epistles), all are divinely inspired.

A friend once shared his concern that I was spending too much time preaching out of the Old Testament. When I inquired why this should be such a concern, he commented that only the Epistles were written to the Church. In his opinion, the Old Testament was filled with stories and was not as essential for us today as the New Testament Epistles. I explained that he was correct when he said that the Epistles were written to the Church, but was not correct in saying that the Old Testament is less important for us today.

Paul told his readers that what had happened to the Israelites in the Old Testament was an example for them, as it is for us today: "Now these things occurred as examples, to keep us from setting our hearts on evil things as they did. . . . These things happened to them as examples and were written down as warnings for us, on whom the fulfillment of the ages has come" (1 Corinthians 10:6,11).

The totality of Scripture is inspired, with no part of Scripture more inspired than another. Though some passages are easier to understand and others are more practical, none are more inspired than others.

A second observation that surfaced as I investigated this passage is that Scripture was divinely initiated. This is why the Bible is so unique when compared to other "holy" books. The Bible alone is generated from God, while all other religious and sacred writings have originated with man. God did not want man to be in the dark concerning His nature and works. Therefore, the Lord revealed Himself to man so that man could understand, appreciate, and worship Him.

The word translated "inspired" derives from two Greek words: *theos*, meaning God, and *pneumatos*, which can be translated breath, wind, or spirit. The totality of Scripture has been breathed by God, a concept that first surfaced during Creation, when God made man. The account states, "The LORD God formed the man from the dust of the ground and breathed into his nostrils the breath of life, and the man became a living being" (Genesis 2:7). When God breathed into man, not only did man experience life, but he also came into existence flawless. In a similar manner, God directed men to write what He revealed to them in various ways. Thus, He "breathed" the Scriptures into many of His followers, who wrote down that message. In this way, Scripture was born in flawless fashion. So the Bible came into existence by the breath of God as He initiated contact with man.

We see a parallel concept in Peter's writings: "Above all, you must understand that no prophecy of Scripture came about by the prophet's own interpretation. For prophecy never had its origin in the will of man, but men spoke from God as they were carried along by the Holy Spirit" (2 Peter 1:20-21). When the prophets spoke, they did not act on their own. In fact, they were very much aware of what might happen to them once they delivered the message. Many were put into prison and tortured, while others lost their lives because they faithfully delivered God's message to the intended recipients.

When visitors come to Orange, we usually give them a tour of the southern California beaches. One of our favorite spots is Dana Point, which is a large harbor housing hundreds of boats. As we walk along the docking area, we watch crafts move slowly in and out of their slips. As they make their way through the harbor toward the ocean, they unfold their sails and catch the wind, which moves them out into the ocean for a beautiful day of sailing.

Paul chose this artistic scene of sails catching the wind and moving a ship toward its destination as an illustration of divine initiation. Like the wind, the Holy Spirit blew into the lives of all the writers, moving them to pen what God wanted to reveal. In the process, God used the specific personalities, education, experience, and styles of these writers, guiding them to produce the inspired book called the Bible.

One further observation concerns the purpose of the Bible, which is divinely designed. Scripture teaches the difference between right and wrong. It provides an objective value system, encouragement, comfort, hope, and wisdom. But this passage indicates that the *purpose* of Scripture is "to equip." Since God wants the believer to be prepared for whatever he will face in life, He equips the believer through teaching, rebuking, correcting, and training. So your waiting room experience is part of that equipping process. He is giving you the opportunity to spend time in His Word so that as you pass through this testing period, you will emerge as one who has matured and is better equipped to handle life's problems. Notice how effective the Bible is in relationship to man's need.

The psalmist testified to the instructional value of affliction: "It was good for me to be afflicted so that I might learn your decrees" (Psalm 119:71). Affliction is a tutor. Sometimes it's more like a hard taskmaster. But we have the opportunity to learn through tough times, and will learn best as the Holy Spirit is allowed to instruct through His Word. God taught me the following lessons during my waiting room experience.

GOD REMAINS IN CONTROL

I knew in theory that God was in control, but while I waited on Him, the theory translated into reality. When I observed the events around me, it looked as though everything was out of control. Conditions were spiraling downward. Setbacks became commonplace. The opposing forces seemed to be winning the ball game. The pitch was two and zero, the bottom of the ninth with two outs, and I was at bat. The chance of me getting any kind of hit was unlikely. I felt that the circumstances were stacked against me. As I looked around for my Manager, He was nowhere in sight. It was time to put my faith into operation. I determined to believe what He said about Himself in His Word. I read the following passages, which convinced me once again that God was in control, whether I felt it or not.

> "Woe to him who quarrels with his Maker, to him who is but a potsherd among the potsherds on the ground. Does the clay say to the potter, 'What are you making?'" (Isaiah 45:9)

> "I make known the end from the beginning, from ancient times, what is still to come. I say: My purpose will stand, and I will do all that I please. . . . What I have said, that will I bring about; what I have planned, that will I do." (Isaiah 46:10-11)

> There is no wisdom, no insight, no plan that can succeed against the LORD. (Proverbs 21:30)

> Many are the plans in a man's heart, but it is the LORD's purpose that prevails. (Proverbs 19:21)

> A man's steps are directed by the LORD. How then can anyone understand his own way? (Proverbs 20:24)

> The king's heart is in the hand of the LORD; he directs it like a watercourse wherever he pleases. (Proverbs 21:1)

According to these verses, there is no doubt who is in control of life. It is easy to fall prey to the attitude that you are losing the battle and everyone else is winning. But according to God's Word, what may be "losing" to you, could very well translate into a great victory.

This means that God's will (desire) and His plan (purpose) are not always synonymous. For instance, God's will is like a finely woven cloth of pure silk. It is always consistent with His character: moral, pure, perfect, and revealed in His Word. But His plan is more like a tapestry of various materials, those that are smooth and those that are very coarse. It includes good and evil; both positive and negative (Job 2:9-10, Isaiah 45:7). God's will includes what He wants to happen, while the Lord's plan includes what He allows to happen, then working the ingredients into His overall purpose. Consider Jesus' ministry in His hometown of Nazareth. He wanted (will) to perform miracles there, but because of the people's unbelief, He chose not to (Mark 6:4-6).

The distinction between God's will and His plan is also illustrated in two statements that Samuel made to King Saul. When the king disobeyed God by usurping the authority of the priest, Samuel rebuked him, saying, "You acted foolishly. . . . You have not kept the command the LORD your God gave you; if you had, he would have established your kingdom over Israel for all time" (God's will) (1 Samuel 13:13). The Lord wanted Saul to remain king over Israel, but He also wanted an obedient king. But when Saul took matters into his own hands by taking authority away from God's anointed priests, Samuel told him the consequences of his actions.

The prophet announced, "But now your kingdom will not endure; the LORD has sought out a man after his own heart and appointed him leader of his people, because you have not kept the LORD's command" (God's plan and purpose) (1 Samuel 13:14). God used Saul's disobedience and worked it into the overall purpose of establishing David as king to reign over Israel. Though Saul did everything in his power to prevent David from ascending to the throne, God's plan succeeded, while Saul's plan failed. Who really won? God, of course.

It was important to be reminded that God was still in control. At times I felt as though everything was out of control. Nothing made much sense. I felt somewhat like Joseph. The more I told the Lord, "I'm willing to do whatever You want," the less I was able to determine the circumstances. And so I slipped further away from my dreams. I needed the next lesson.

GOD CAN BRING GOOD OUT OF EVIL

I reminded myself on many occasions of that familiar passage: "We know that in all things God works for the good of those who love him, who have been called according to his purpose" (Romans 8:28). The "all things" includes those difficult people, those plans that fall apart, the ideas that cannot be initiated, and the physical limitations due to sickness, surgery, and accidents. God is able to take the very problems I face and bring good results, as He did in the case of Joseph.

Man is always held accountable for his actions. Judas was responsible for betraying Jesus, but God used that betrayal to generate salvation for all who will call upon the name of Jesus. Those who crucified the Lord are accountable for putting Him to death, and yet listen to the results: "This man was handed over to you by God's set purpose and foreknowledge; and you, with the help of wicked men, put him to death by nailing him to the cross. . . . God has raised this Jesus to life, and we are all witnesses of the fact. Exalted to the right hand of God, he has received from the Father the promised Holy Spirit and has poured out what you now see and hear" (Acts 2:23,32-33). God was able to use man's jealousy, anger, and cruelty to make salvation and the Holy Spirit available to those who believe.

GOD CARES FOR THOSE WHO ARE HURTING

The Lord does not stand by as an apathetic observer. He is involved in our problems. He understands our hurts. The writer to the Hebrews verified this truth when he wrote, "We do not have a high priest who is unable to sympathize with our weaknesses, but we have one who has been tempted in every way, just as we are—yet was without sin. Let us then approach the throne of grace with confidence, so that we may receive mercy and find grace to help us in our time of need" (Hebrews 4:15,16).

At times, our cries for help may seem to fall on deaf ears, but God hears our cries and even now may be in the process of responding. The passage of Scripture that sent this concept to my troubled soul was from the prophet Isaiah, who said about Israel, "In all their distress he too was distressed" (Isaiah 63:9). That insight into God's emotional involvement in my life was like a cup of cold water to a thirsty man. It quenched many of my questions about God's care for me.

WAITING IS ACTIVE RATHER THAN PASSIVE

Also, I discovered that I don't have to wait by sitting on my hands and staring out the window, hoping for an opportunity to come walking down some lonely path. Though many things are out of our reach, we can take some logical steps as we wait.

While Joseph waited in prison for God's next chapter of his life, he was busy taking care of various duties under his responsibility (Genesis 39:20-23). While David waited for the time when he would ascend to the throne, he spent a lot of his time writing many of the psalms we read today. He also developed a team of supporters, known later as "David's mighty men" (2 Samuel 23:8-39). While the disciples waited for the promised Holy Spirit, they went to the upper room and spent their time replacing Judas with Matthias and praying (Acts 1).

Ask yourself, "What can I do as I wait for the Lord?" Is there someone to contact? Do you need to seek out counsel? What person needs to hear from you or needs your encouragement? What ministry opportunity is not being fulfilled because no one is available? Who is hurting that you can help?

GOD DESIRES TO GIVE YOU WHAT YOU NEED, BUT NOT ALWAYS WHAT YOU WANT

Children are notorious for wanting things, and teenagers tend to confuse their wants with their needs. How often have mothers of teens heard their daughters complain, "But Mom, I need a new dress. I don't have a thing to wear to the party tonight!" We smile at our children, who feel they need everything they want. But we fail to realize that our discernment isn't much better. It takes a lot of discipline to resist the "buy now, pay later" philosophy that surrounds us. That new house, car, TV, computer, or video camera seem so essential to our life. We are certain that we just can't function without it. But time proves us wrong. When the creditors send letters of demand for late payments and there's too much month left at the end of the money, we acknowledge with embarrassment that we probably should have waited. What we thought we needed could easily have been postponed to a later date.

Self-deception is not limited to material things. We

believe that we know what is best for us in other areas of life. We want security, good health, and success. We want to be self-reliant, and would like everything in life to run smoothly. We want our children to be happy and free from the many struggles we had to encounter when we were young. But are these the qualities of life that are best for us?

God may want to evict us from our comfort zone so that we will learn to depend upon Him. He may see that we need humility in place of pride, dependency on Him instead of self-reliance, and a taste of failure rather than continuous success. When the roof caves in, we may cry out, "I didn't need that!" But the Lord may be saying from heaven, "Yes you did. That's why I gave it to you." If God gave us only what was good and pleasant, we would never become the quality people into which He wants to shape us.

The instructional value of affliction and Scripture go hand in hand. Affliction leads us to God's Word, and the Bible provides us a context from which we can see our circumstances more clearly and make wise decisions. Along with the instructional benefits of Scripture, one could add the value of rebuking.

SCRIPTURE IS USEFUL FOR REBUKING

No one likes to be rebuked. We appreciate compliments and encouragement, but not rebuke. Why? Because rebuke points out the weaknesses in our lives. It says, "This is wrong for you. Get your life straightened out." I recall vivid memories of being rebuked by my teachers in grade school, and a few terrifying experiences of being sent down to the principal's office for disciplinary purposes when I was in high school. As I sat outside his office, the clock on the wall grew louder by the minute, ticking the passing seconds that were about to usher in the wrath of the principal.

To be rebuked means being told "No." Some children may wonder if their name is "No." They hear parents, siblings and teachers tell them, "No, don't touch that." "No, don't take that. It doesn't belong to you." "No, you can't have the car tonight." "No, you can't stay out until one o'clock in the morning."

Then, even after they are grown and responsible for their own decisions and actions, they continue to hear someone telling them, "No." Only this time it is neither their teacher nor their parents, but the Word of God. God rebukes through His Word because man deviates from His declared will. Sometimes the rebuke will come through the Word, while at other times it may come through an individual. The Bible records a variety of rebukes.

The prophet Samuel rebuked King Saul (1 Samuel 10:8, 13:7-14). Another prophet rebuked King Asa (2 Chronicles 16:7-9). Micaiah rebuked King Ahab (2 Chronicles 18:5-7,25-27). Nathan the prophet rebuked King David (2 Samuel 12:1-13). The apostle Peter rebuked Simon the sorcerer (Acts 8:14-23) and the apostle Paul rebuked Peter (Galatians 2:11-21).

Rebuke may not be pleasant, but it is necessary. The Bible states, "A rebuke impresses a man of discernment more than a hundred lashes a fool" (Proverbs 17:10). Some people never profit from a rebuke. Instead, they either respond in anger or justify their actions. But a wise person is teachable and will learn much from a reprimand. Even though he may not like the admonition when it first comes, he will benefit from it in time.

On many occasions I have been reproved by the Scriptures. Sometimes the chiding has centered on an attitude that needed changing. At other moments it's what I've said or what I've done. In either case, the rebuke was necessary, though not always welcomed.

SCRIPTURE IS USEFUL FOR CORRECTION

In His grace, God not only rebukes by telling us where we are out of line, but He also shows us the way back to the right path. Some people are self-appointed critics of everyone else's life. Their purpose is not to improve the situation. Instead, they just want to point out everything that, in their opinion, is wrong. Nothing constructive. They are not willing to become part of the solution, so in the process they become much of the problem. They often set a standard for others that they themselves fail to keep. They are guilty of what Jesus pointed out to the religious leaders of His day when He chided, "The teachers of the law and the Pharisees sit in Moses' seat. So you must obey them and do everything they tell you. But do not do what they do, for they do not practice what they preach" (Matthew 23:1-3).

God is not like that. Whenever He says something is wrong, He also points out how to correct the problem. Notice the following corrections for wrong living:

> Do not conform any longer to the pattern of this world, but be transformed by the renewing of your mind. (Romans 12:2)

> Do not think of yourself more highly than you ought, but rather think of yourself with sober judgment, in accordance with the measure of faith God has given you. (Romans 12:3)

> Do not be proud, but be willing to associate with people of low position. (Romans 12:16)

> Do not take revenge, my friends, but leave room for God's wrath, for it is written: "It is mine to avenge; I

will repay," says the Lord. (Romans 12:19)

Do not get drunk on wine, which leads to debauchery. Instead, be filled with the Spirit. (Ephesians 5:18)

Do nothing out of selfish ambition or vain conceit, but in humility consider others better than yourselves. Each of you should look not only to your own interests, but also to the interests of others. (Philippians 2:3-4)

Do not be anxious about anything, but in everything, by prayer and petition, with thanksgiving, present your requests to God. (Philippians 4:6)

The Scriptures don't leave the reader in the dark. You don't have to guess what God wants you to do when He tells you to stop following your present course of action.

Each of the above passages helped me during my own inner struggles. Whenever negative feelings toward people arose in my life, I would be reminded that they are answerable to God. He knows my heart and is aware of why they do what they do. I neither have to judge nor get even with them. Instead, I can leave the results with God. The Scriptures are profitable for teaching, rebuking, and correction. But they are also useful for training.

SCRIPTURE IS USEFUL FOR
TRAINING IN RIGHTEOUSNESS

The word translated "training" in 2 Timothy 3:16 is the Greek *paideia*, meaning upbringing, training, or instruction. It is used to describe the process of training or disciplining children. Children must be taught to distinguish between right and wrong. And part of that teaching process includes discipline.

Children do not know what they do not know. They are oblivious to the dangers around them. They live with the false assumption that they are in control of life's situations. So they tend to become an accident looking for a place to happen. Unfortunately, adults follow a similar pattern. We may have the knowledge of right and wrong, but not necessarily the personal discipline to put that knowledge to work in our lives.

The early Church was not composed of all mature, Spirit-filled believers. That's why the writer to the Hebrews gave this message to his readers:

> We have much to say about this, but it is hard to explain because you are slow to learn. In fact, though by this time you ought to be teachers, you need someone to teach you the elementary truths of God's word all over again. You need milk, not solid food! Anyone who lives on milk, being still an infant, is not acquainted with the teaching about righteousness. But solid food is for the mature, who by constant use have trained themselves to distinguish good from evil. (Hebrews 5:11-14)

These believers were Christians long enough to have qualified as teachers of younger converts. Yet they did not have the spiritual credentials to teach. A person fighting the "battle of the bulge" may purchase a stationary bike for the purpose of exercise and weight loss. After several months, he should show signs of progress. But if he never gets on the bike, he will be in no better physical shape than before he purchased the bike. Likewise, the believer who has known the Lord for many years, but has failed to relate the Bible to everyday living, also will not be spiritually fit to teach others.

One of my joys in life is racquetball. I don't play tournament ball, but I can usually hold my own with average players. Often I'll play men ten to fifteen years my junior and beat them, even though they are better players than I. My secret weapon is conditioning. That's where the jogging comes in handy. By constant running, my body remains conditioned to play racquetball. So when I play fellows younger than myself, they will often take the first game or two. But I go for the marathon, adding many games to our afternoon. Eventually my young opponents wear down and get careless. Of course, now that my secret weapon has been exposed, I've probably ended my racquetball career.

Training in righteousness is a process accomplished by spiritual conditioning: giving constant attention to Scripture and putting its truth into everyday life. The more we saturate ourselves with God's Word, the better equipped we will be in the ways of wholesome living.

When I was a teenager, some of my friends invited me to explore a cave. As we inched our way through the darkness, clinging to the damp, cold walls of the cave, we entered an area that had a small opening, just large enough for a person to crawl through. With only one flashlight between us, we allowed the guy with the light to lead us. After about a half-hour in the cave, the flashlight flickered, dimmed, and then went out. Suddenly the excitement of exploration began to give way to panic. We bombarded each other with a lot of rhetorical questions: "How are we going to get out of here?" "Does anybody know we are here?" "How long do you think we can last in this cave without food or water?"

After about ten minutes of doom and gloom forecasting, one of us came up with the brilliant idea of banging the flashlight against a rock, hoping to jar the batteries into making a connection. After several attempts the flashlight flickered and the light returned. However, it was only about one-fourth as bright as before. But that was enough to find that small opening again, climb through and scurry out of the cave. The flashlight was our only hope of getting out of the cave unharmed.

The psalmist perceived the Scriptures in a similar way when he wrote, "Your word is a lamp to my feet and a light for my path" (Psalm 119:105). To neglect the Bible as we live in a world of spiritual darkness makes as much sense as trying to walk through a dark cave with a flashlight in hand but never turning it on. It does explain why some Christians stumble and fall constantly, hurting themselves and others in the process. It makes more sense to keep the light turned on so that we can see where we are going.

8
The Dynamic of Prayer

As I write this chapter I am sitting alone at a lake cabin. My wife and the couple with whom we are staying are out for a walk. Alongside me is my trusted companion, Champ, a three-legged, fifteen-year-old beagle who has never before seen a lake. Every scent that reaches him promises a fresh and exciting adventure.

On the floor Champ lies with his head between his paws. While staring at the trees and the lake, he hears the sound of two courting Minnesota loons echoing from off the water. Though the sounds are new to him, he is neither startled nor disturbed. His ears lift a little, but then lower, as a serenity descends upon him, carrying him into a dream world understood only by another beagle. What a perfect picture of "man's best friend" at peace with himself and the world around him.

But have you ever wondered why we call this species of the animal kingdom "man's best friend"? Think for a moment how a dog can make just about anyone feel good. As far as he is concerned, you are number one in his life. He greets you at the door with his tail swinging from side to side. Whether your day has been relaxed or hectic, he gives you his undivided attention. If you want to tell him how badly people have treated you, he'll stare you in the eyes with an empathetic expression, communicating, "Go ahead and tell me what's on your mind. After all, what are friends for?"

A dog patiently listens to your complaints, hurts, future plans, and great successes. You can tell him anything, and he seems to understand. So it's not hard to see why he's honored as man's best friend.

Well, I don't want to disillusion you, but the fact of the matter is that your wonderful friend and my fifteen-year-old beagle understand little of what we confide in them. But that's okay. We love them anyway, and will probably continue to confide in them.

But the good news is that there's a "best friend" who understands every thought, every emotion, and every word. That friend promises to be available at all times, for He has said, "Never will I leave you; never will I forsake you" (Hebrews 13:5). The psalmist testifies that this friend knows you better than you know yourself:

O LORD, you have searched me and you know me. You know when I sit and when I rise; you perceive my thoughts from afar. You discern my going out and my lying down; you are familiar with all my ways. Before a word is on my tongue you know it completely, O LORD. You hem me in—behind and before; you have laid your hand upon me. Such knowledge is too wonderful for me, too lofty for me to attain. (Psalm 139:1-6)

God wants to become your best friend. You are so important to Him that He developed a special plan that would allow you to spend an eternity with Him—a plan that cost Him the life of His only Son. And in spite of the tremendous personal cost, He felt you were worth it.

You can tell God anything you want, including your doubts, frustrations, fears, excitement, grief, desires, and how you really feel inside. He not only hears what you are saying, but He also wants to do something about your situation. The Lord is able to comfort the hurting spirit, mend the broken relationship, revive the weary soul, impart wisdom to the confused mind, and infuse faith into the doubting heart.

Praying while you wait is not optional. Without it, you could feel like a victim of circumstances, which is not what He wants for you. Paul encouraged, "Do not be anxious about anything, but in everything, by prayer and petition, with thanksgiving, present your requests to God. And the peace of God, which transcends all understanding, will guard your hearts and your minds in Christ Jesus" (Philippians 4:6-7). The word translated "prayer" refers to prayer in general, while "petition" speaks of specific requests. And "thanksgiving" is the attitude of the heart when presenting your requests to the Lord. Such praying acknowledges God as the one in control and yourself as a thankful recipient of God's grace.

When I feel that I am totally responsible for the outcome of circumstances, I cannot help but sense anxiety. Many circumstances are within my ability to change, but what can I do with those situations beyond my control? Nothing. Therefore, why live in a state of anxiety over such events? God offers me both a response to my petitions and His peace. But that's not the only reason we need to pray. Let's investigate the matter further.

When the whole world seems to be caving in and you feel like you're up to your armpits in alligators, prayer does not always surface to the conscious mind as the most logical step to take. Panic or despair would seem more natural. However, they lead only to greater difficulty in the future. The better response is to pray. I say this for two major reasons. The first is what prayer does for you, and the second is what it does for the problem you face.

PRAYER BRINGS YOU INTO THE VERY PRESENCE OF GOD

Entering into the presence of God may not appear at first to be very special. After all, we've never seen God, so what can we expect? But a few individuals have had that privilege, and when they saw the Lord, they did not glibly present Him with a long grocery list of petitions. Consider Isaiah's intense reaction as he caught a glimpse of heaven's focus for worship:

> In the year that King Uzziah died, I saw the Lord seated on a throne, high and exalted, and the train of his robe filled the temple. Above him were seraphs, each with six wings: With two wings they covered their faces, with two they covered their feet, and with two they were flying. And they were calling to one another: "Holy, holy, holy is the LORD Almighty; the whole earth is full of his glory." At the sound of their voices the doorposts and thresholds shook and the temple was filled with smoke. "Woe to me!" I cried. "I am ruined! For I am a man of unclean lips, and I live among a people of unclean lips, and my eyes have seen the King, the LORD Almighty." (Isaiah 6:1-5)

The prophet was humbled at the sight of a holy God, and immediately recognized his own sinfulness.

Many of us would be ecstatic if we were invited by the President of the United States to his Oval Office. And we would be even more pleased if he gave us the entire day to ask him any questions we wanted and then promised to help us in whatever area we needed his help. We would be the envy of everyone in the neighborhood and at work.

Well, that opportunity will probably never come to either you or me, but a similar and far more impressive option has been left open to us. God calls us into His private chambers and allows us to spend as much time as we want, pouring out our needs, and then He promises to give us whatever is best for us. That's an offer difficult for anyone to refuse. Yet most people do exactly that: refuse His generous offer. But consider what we turn down when we neglect to accept God's invitation.

God is the most powerful person with whom you will ever speak. He possesses the power over life and death, victory and defeat. All creation is subject to God's power, including angels, demons, nature, animal life, and man. David boasted in the power of God, saying, "In my distress I called to the LORD; I cried to my God for help. From his temple he heard my voice; my cry came before him, into his ears. . . . He reached down from on high and took hold of me; he drew me out of deep waters" (Psalm 18:6, 16). Paul rested in the same power, stating, "I can do everything through him who gives me strength" (Philippians 4:13). And the testimony of the Lord verifies this truth: "With man this is impossible, but with God all things are possible" (Matthew 19:26). What impossible situation do you face? With what impossible person do you have to deal? Why not bring your need to the most powerful person in existence?

God is the most generous person with whom you will ever

speak. In a world full of self-seeking people, it is always refreshing to run into someone who has a beneficent spirit, always doing for others; constantly providing for others; faithfully giving to others. But such individuals are few and far between. However, for all of their magnanimity, these good Samaritans cannot compare with the generosity of God, who gives us the very breath we breathe. How strange that man usually views God as someone who wants to take all the fun out of life and make life miserable. Few people recognize all the Lord has given them, and fewer still understand that He has so much more He wants to give to those willing to acknowledge Him as Lord of their lives.

God is the most concerned person with whom you will ever speak. It is not easy to find people who are concerned for your welfare. Oh, you can probably count on family members and a few friends, but most people are concerned more for their own welfare. Jesus raised an interesting question to His hearers as they sat on the mountainside, listening attentively: "Which of you, if his son asks for bread, will give him a stone? Or if he asks for a fish, will give him a snake?" (Matthew 7:9-10).

Fathers are naturally concerned for their children. When they observe a legitimate need, they will do whatever they can to help. If a son asks for bread, no loving father will make fun of his need and give him a stone instead, or a snake in place of a fish. The Lord continues His story and compares earthly fathers to our heavenly Father: "If you, then, though you are evil, know how to give good gifts to your children, how much more will your Father in heaven give good gifts to those who ask him!" (Matthew 7:11). The Lord is concerned about you. He knows the difficulties you've faced. He is aware of your struggles. But He also wants you to ask Him to meet those needs and then trust Him to do so.

God is the most available person with whom you will ever speak. Availability is something most of us have too little to share. When our sons were in their formative years, our older son, Rick, had a crib and our younger son, Steven, had a bed with a rail to prevent him from rolling out. I don't know why we never thought of rearranging the boys, because Rick never budged when he was sleeping but Steven was all over the bed, often landing on the floor. I slept very lightly and could be awakened by the smallest sound because my mind was focused on the rattle of the bar as Steven was about to plunge to the floor. In all of those early years, I believe I missed catching him in midair only once. All of the other times I was able to jump out of bed, run down the hall, and either stop him or catch him as he rolled off his bed. That's what you call availability.

The word *trust* means to roll on. That is exactly what God wants us to do when we are troubled, confused, desperate, or just looking for guidance: to "roll on Him." He is available twenty-four hours each day. His eyes and ears are focused on us. He knows that in spite of the rails of protection He gives us in the form of warnings, laws, and principles, we will at times go over them and plunge downward to our own hurt. Therefore, it is to our advantage to accept His availability and "roll into His arms." Or as Moses put it, "The eternal God is your refuge, and underneath are the everlasting arms" (Deuteronomy 33:27).

GOD CAN DO SOMETHING ABOUT THE PROBLEM

A second reason to pray is that the Lord is not only available, but He also is able. The circumstances may be out of hand. Perhaps everything has been tried, but still the difficulty persists. Be assured you are not alone. Others have also faced impossible situations and have experienced some resounding results. Consider one example: a man named Jehoshaphat, King of Judah.

A vast army had swept across the country and was almost on the doorsteps of Jerusalem. Jehoshaphat and the people realized they had little chance for victory. The king responded to the impossible odds by proclaiming a fast for all of Judah, and together the people came to inquire of God. The Judean king confessed, "O our God, will you not judge them? For we have no power to face this vast army that is attacking us. We do not know what to do, but our eyes are upon you" (2 Chronicles 20:12).

At first, Jehoshaphat's position may appear to be one of weakness, but in reality it was one of strength. Any time we are forced into a situation where we have to look to the Lord, we are in a position of strength because we recognize the insufficient resources of our own ability. This is when God has the opportunity to demonstrate to us what He can do.

The Lord spoke to the king through a man named Jahaziel, who said, "Listen, King Jehoshaphat and all who live in Judah and Jerusalem! This is what the LORD says to you: 'Do not be afraid or discouraged because of this vast army. For the battle is not yours, but God's. . . . You will not have to fight this battle'" (2 Chronicles 20:15,17).

Sometimes the Lord leads us to do something about the issue at hand, but other times He tells us to step aside and allow Him to fight the battle for us. The more we are tuned in to God, the better opportunity we have to discern whether we should fight or step back and let the Lord handle it. In either case, God will intervene when we enter His presence in holiness and expectation, seeking His direction.

But sometimes when we pray, God responds with an answer of *no*. At such times we may feel like a child being rejected by his parents. But we shouldn't, because the Lord has good reasons why He withholds from us. Consider the prayer requests of some of the greatest believers in history, including the Son of God.

God said no to Moses. Why? Because of a disobedient act. When God told Moses to speak to the rock so that the Lord could provide water for the people, Moses disobeyed by striking the rock twice with his staff. God rebuked Moses on the spot by saying, "Because you did not trust in me enough to honor me as holy in the sight of the Israelites, you will not bring this community into the land I give them" (Numbers 20:12).

Years later, when Moses and the people were preparing to cross the Jordan into the land of promise, Moses pleaded with God for the opportunity to enter the new land. After all, this was what he had worked for during the past forty years of his life. This was his vision, his goal in life: to lead Israel from bondage to freedom and into a land of plenty. But note how God responded to Moses' request.

"'That is enough,' the LORD said. 'Do not speak to me anymore about this matter. Go up to the top of Pisgah and look west and north and south and east. Look at the land with your own eyes, since you are not going to cross this Jordan. But commission Joshua, and encourage and strengthen him, for he will lead this people across and will cause them to inherit the land that you will see'" (Deuteronomy 3:26-28).

There are those times in life when we ask God for a specific need or desire but He does not give us what we ask for because of our disobedient heart. Just as parents are not prone to give their children what they want when they have been disobedient, neither does God bless His own when they willfully disobey.

God refused David's prayer request for an entirely

different reason. Have you ever wanted to do something for God that you thought would honor Him greatly, and yet it just didn't work out? This is what happened to David. He wanted to build a Temple for the Lord. It was not a selfish desire, but rather a God-honoring intention. However, it was not in God's plan for David to build the Temple. The king recalled the events of the period as he addressed the people:

> "Listen to me, my brothers and my people. I had it in my heart to build a house as a place of rest for the ark of the covenant of the LORD, for the footstool of our God, and I made plans to build it. But God said to me, 'You are not to build a house for my Name, because you are a warrior and have shed blood.' . . . He said to me: 'Solomon your son is the one who will build my house and my courts, for I have chosen him to be my son, and I will be his father.'"
> (1 Chronicles 28:2-3,6)

Hence, David did not build the Temple. And yet the Lord allowed him to begin the process. David drew up the architectural plans for the Temple given to him by the Holy Spirit (1 Chronicles 28:11-19), commissioned his son to do the building (28:20), organized part of the work force (28:21), and raised the capital (29:1-9). Like Moses, David had the opportunity to begin the work, but not to finish it.

To be in this position is difficult. Pastors experience it often. One man lays a great foundation of ministry and another comes in and reaps the benefits of it. In my Fresno ministry, I had the privilege of turning over a ministry to another pastor, who has reaped the benefits of what took me thirteen years to build. Today I have inherited the work of another pastor's ten-year investment. Some projects that

I could not complete in Fresno my successor could, while certain goals that my predecessor did not achieve, I now have the opportunity to fulfill. Certain requests may be God-honoring and very unselfish, but not necessarily part of God's plan and purpose. He may say no, and yet at the same time honor you for your intention.

God refused to say yes to the apostle Paul's request for healing. Instead, the Lord told Paul, "My grace is sufficient for you, for my power is made perfect in weakness" (2 Corinthians 12:9). There are those times when God withholds the answer we are looking for, and yet He will not leave us destitute. For Paul, God's grace was a much better answer than His healing. What we think is best may be second-rate when compared with what God knows is best.

One further example of the Lord not granting a request is the account of His own Son's prayer when Jesus asked, "Father, if you are willing, take this cup from me; yet not my will, but yours be done" (Luke 22:42). God the Father did not remove the cup. Instead, Jesus tasted the grief of rejection and the pain of death. In the process, He gained more than He lost and made it possible for man to receive forgiveness and life eternal.

It is important to realize that a "no" answer is not always bad, and often is better for us. Perhaps the greatest no answer I received from the Lord was when I prayed very sincerely and regularly that He would salvage the situation in my Minnesota ministry. I prayed that He would turn things around so that I might continue to serve the people I had grown to love so dearly. But circumstances only grew worse. Every time I thought I saw a turnaround, something would surface to assure me that the breakthrough was temporary.

For a while I wondered why the Lord would say no to such a proper request. After all, this was Christ's church, and I knew He wanted His people to live in harmony with one another and love one another. But the answer was not one of revival, restoration, and moving ahead. The darkest days were still ahead. The Lord finally made it clear that as long as I remained as senior pastor, the issues that needed to surface would not. So God said no, and His plan continued to unfold as He probed, pruned, and purged.

How should you react when the Lord closes the door to your request? Should you think you have somehow offended God? Should you feel rejected by the One who promised never to leave you? Should you become angry with God?

HOW SHOULD YOU RESPOND TO A "NO" ANSWER?

How should you respond when you wait and pray, but don't receive what you are looking for? Here are four suggestions:

First, do not attempt to coerce God into giving you the request. Children have a tendency to do that to their parents. They like to play one parent against the other. If one says no, the child runs to the other with the same request. God doesn't play those games. When He makes it clear that the answer is no, any attempt to manipulate Him or make some deal with Him is futile. It's a waste of energy and time, and it prevents you from receiving God's best.

Second, attempt to understand why He said no. For instance, here are some possible questions to ask:

• What might the Lord be trying to teach you about yourself, others, or Himself in this situation?
• Is there an area of your life that needs to be changed, such as an attitude, the way you relate to people, the use of your tongue, how you are handling your finances, or how you treat your spouse?
• Could the Lord be trying to point out another

option you've not yet considered? What might that
option be?
• Is it possible that He wants to spare you some
future problems? What might they be?
• Could He want to do something much greater or
more significant than what you are requesting? What
might that be?

Third, acknowledge God as Lord. Jesus, the Lord, has
full control over all our circumstances and possesses the
right to do as He pleases with our lives. Many times I do not
understand what He is doing or why He is doing it. Sometimes that's really bothersome. When I ponder the fact that
Jesus has my best interests at heart, I can relax more and
worry less about how He is going to make it all work out
properly.

When I was writing this chapter, I was waiting for God's
next ministry assignment. As I evaluated the events that led
to a letter of resignation, I discovered a number of options
lying before me. I could have been bitter. I might have
attempted to get even with those who were responsible. I
could have joined the ranks of the Church's walking
wounded, spending weeks mourning the loss of what might
have been. However, I rejected all of these options because
none of them declared the sovereign right of the Lord Jesus
Christ to do as He pleases, even if it means using man's
wrong intentions or improper conduct to accomplish His
purposes. The Lord knows how to discipline those who
need it, and He knows how to guide those who are willing to
be led by His Holy Spirit.

As a senior pastor I could not view the church as my
own, for the Lord Jesus never abandoned His claim, "I will
build my church." I continue to see myself as a servant of
the Lord Jesus Christ on assignment. When the assignment

is finished according to His purpose, I must be prepared to accept another assignment, no matter what or where that might be. This philosophy is not easy to follow, but it is essential to accept. So I encourage you, don't deny Him the right to do with you as He pleases.

A final suggestion is to accept His answer of no with thanksgiving, knowing that His way is best. The Lord impressed on me these words of Isaiah during my days of waiting: "The LORD will guide you always; he will satisfy your needs in a sun-scorched land and will strengthen your frame. You will be like a well-watered garden, like a spring whose waters never fail" (Isaiah 58:11).

Today I minister in the sun-scorched land of California. God has satisfied my needs in so many ways and has indeed strengthened my frame. My health is better than it has been in years, my weight is about where it should be, and He has restored to me the joy of ministry. On top of all this, the Lord is in the process of richly blessing my ministry in a new and satisfying way. I never thought that I'd be thankful when God turned down my request to keep me where I was and bring about revival under my leadership, but today I can say, "Thank You, Lord. Even when I questioned Your wisdom and was confused by Your refusal to answer me as I had asked, I thank You that You had something better in mind. Amen."

HOW TO PRAY EFFECTIVELY WHILE WAITING

Praying while waiting becomes a real test of faith. You so desperately want to see something happen. You want action. But often it just doesn't happen. Heaven seems to be filled with silence. The days, weeks, and months may pass without any great evidence that God is at work. Remember, perception and reality are not always the same. God may be in the process of answering your prayers at this very moment, but for one reason or another, the answer may be delayed. Consider the following four directives for effective prayer while you wait.

First, *recognize that you are in a spiritual battle.* Paul informed his readers, "Our struggle is not against flesh and blood, but against the rulers, against the authorities, against the powers of this dark world and against the spiritual forces of evil in the heavenly realms" (Ephesians 6:12). Daniel experienced a three-week delay in his answer due to Satanic opposition (Daniel 10:2), and so did the apostle Paul (1 Thessalonians 2:18). The Christian life is not lived in a vacuum, but in a war zone. And the greater the commitment to Christ, the more one can expect spiritual warfare to increase.

Second, *pray for God's will to be accomplished.* I know some people see this as a cop out, and perhaps we are guilty at times of covering up our lack of faith by praying, "If it is Your will." On the other hand, this is the way Jesus addressed His Father when He prayed, "Yet not my will, but yours be done" (Luke 22:42).

When we do not apply God's will in our decision making, we border on presumption, which James warned against when he wrote, "Now listen, you who say, 'Today or tomorrow we will go to this or that city, spend a year there, carry on business and make money.' Why, you do not even know what will happen tomorrow. What is your life? You are a mist that appears for a little while and then vanishes. Instead, you ought to say, 'If it is the Lord's will, we will live and do this or that.' As it is, you boast and brag. All such boasting is evil" (James 4:13-16).

We must come to that place where, after we pour out our hearts to the Lord and tell Him our desire, we unconditionally say, "Yet not my will, but Yours be done." When we sincerely pray this way, we can be certain that God will answer according to His will (1 John 5:14).

Third, *pray with perseverance.* It is easy to become discouraged when you pray over a period of time and nothing seems to happen. You feel like throwing in the towel and even begin to wonder if God is really hearing you at all.

An excellent example of persevering in prayer is Elijah. He prayed for rain, but the rain did not come. He continued to ask God for the rain and sent his servant to see if clouds were starting to form in the sky. But still there was no sign of moisture. He prayed like this seven times. Soon a little cloud could be seen over the horizon coming toward the prophet. Elijah rejoiced that the answer was on the way and told his servant, "Go and tell Ahab, 'Hitch up your chariot and go down before the rain stops you'" (1 Kings 18:44). From that little cloud, the prophet could envision a massive thunderstorm, speeding its way to the land that had been plagued by a three-and-a-half year drought.

Is there some small cloud forming over the horizon in your life? If you feel parched and dry because you've been praying for a long time and no answer has come forth, maybe you just need to look around. The cloud may be forming. Moisture may be gathering. Don't give up your prayer life. Keep at it. The rain of refreshment may be on the way.

Riding on the coattails of the last principle is the concept of faith. *When you pray, expect results.* Believe that God will do something in response to your prayer. James warns that faithless prayer results in nothing (James 1:5-7). On the other hand, Jesus promised, "Whatever you ask for in prayer, believe that you have received it, and it will be yours" (Mark 11:24).

Spending time in God's waiting room by yourself is almost unbearable. Having a friend by your side makes the waiting tolerable. And when you devote yourself to prayer while you are waiting, you develop the certainty that you are not alone. God is with you to encourage, comfort, and strengthen you. He is at your side guiding your decisions and filling your mind with His thoughts. And you need His thoughts while you wait because you may have some very important decisions to make in the near future.

9

The Decision-Making Process

Have you ever wondered what goes on in the cockpit of an airliner while you are looking for your seat, putting away carry-on baggage, and strapping yourself into the seat? A friend who flies for one of the major airlines took me through the checklist every pilot must go through. There are about one hundred check points that one pilot reads aloud while the other responds aloud.

They examine more than a dozen items before they start the engines. Then there are more reviews before they taxi to the end of the runway, before they take off, right after they've taken off, when they prepare for a landing, while they are landing, after they have landed, and after they've turned off the engines. And yet in the fatal flight of a Northwest Airlines plane in August 1987, concern was raised that possible failure to check whether the flaps were in the proper position at takeoff may have contributed to the crash. Each point of inspection has been meticulously designed to provide the greatest amount of safety. Failure to follow those checks can lead to catastrophe.

Similar checks are needed when one is making life-changing decisions. Decision-making is difficult enough when life is treating you well, but when the pressure is on and the storm clouds are building, one can fall into the trap of making an emotional rather than a logical decision.

An acquaintance of mine lost his wife through death. Soon after her death, he made an emotional decision to remarry quickly, against the advice of many friends. Today he is divorced.

A young man left his ministry in the Midwest to serve as a youth pastor in the West. He told the search committee of the new church that God had made it clear: He was to serve the Lord with them. And so he gave that church a minimum five-year commitment. Six weeks after he and his family moved across the country and began his new ministry, a position in his former church opened, a position he had desired even before he left. Unknown to the pastor and board of the new church, this young man flew back to his former place of service, met with the pastor, staff, some parents and elders, and within two weeks packed his belongings, his family, and his commitment, and drove across country to take up the new position. When asked by the pastor, parents, board members, and the young people of the church in the West why he was returning to his former church, he replied, "I feel the Lord is leading me back."

Is this the way God really leads a person? Has God left us without any guidelines or checkpoints to follow when we are facing some major decisions in our lives? Are we to rely solely on "gut feelings" or what looks like a better offer to determine the Lord's direction in life? Absolutely not. Like the airline pilot, every believer has been given a number of checkpoints to evaluate as he makes his decisions. The following seven guidelines helped me as I waited on the Lord and made some life-changing decisions.

DISCERN WITH SCRIPTURE

The Bible is not only profitable as a source of great encouragement when you are hurting, but it is also the ultimate resource when you are attempting to discern what God wants you to do. The Scriptures testify to their own value for wisdom in the book of Proverbs. Here's how the book opens:

> The proverbs of Solomon son of David, king of Israel: for attaining wisdom and discipline; for understanding words of insight; for acquiring a disciplined and prudent life, doing what is right and just and fair; for giving prudence to the simple, knowledge and discretion to the young—let the wise listen and add to their learning, and let the discerning get guidance. (Proverbs 1:1-5)

In what ways does the Bible provide discernment? It gives guidance to those who want to enter into a binding partnership. The Scriptures direct, "Do not be yoked together with unbelievers. For what do righteousness and wickedness have in common? Or what fellowship can light have with darkness?" (2 Corinthians 6:14). The yoke was a contraption used to unite two oxen or another pair of animals for the purpose of plowing a field or for hauling produce. If the oxen were not properly trained to work together and each was determined to go his own way, chaos would result.

Today, one can have an unequal yoke in many ways.

Paul refers to the kind of yoke where two individuals differ spiritually, with one knowing the Lord and the other having no relationship with Him at all. Because of this disparity, whenever spiritual issues arise or biblical values surface in their relationship, it will be difficult to work in harmony with one another.

There is also the unequal yoke of vision, direction, goals, methods, personalities, etc. Before any binding relationship is established, it is imperative that both parties know each other and are convinced that they will agree to work out their disagreements.

Partnerships are often formed because one person has money to invest and the other has a good idea. And marriage partners are chosen often without ever discussing the real issues of life such as spiritual habits, how each reacts to problems, how each will handle the finances, personal values, ambitions in life, and other pertinent aspects that influence a relationship.

The Scriptures also provide much wisdom concerning the handling of one's finances, how to get along with others, moral standards, where God fits into problems and solutions, and other such issues. I used the Scriptures to help form my decisions by observing how God worked in the lives of other men.

When I was assured through His Word that God would indeed provide for my needs, I felt more secure about launching out from my comfort zone and entering into the realm of the unknown. My security was no longer in a job, a church, or a geographical location. I came to the place of complete abandonment to whatever God wanted, wherever He wanted me to go. I was reminded of that chorus, "I'm Yours, Lord, everything I've got, everything I am, everything I'm not. I'm Yours, Lord. Try me now and see. See if I can be completely Yours."

DISCERN WITH PRAYER

When the prophets and teachers in the first century Antioch church wanted to send men into other parts of the world with the gospel, they held a prayer meeting. They wanted to get the Lord's work accomplished, but also desired to send those whom the Lord had chosen. So they brought the matter before God in prayer and received the following response from the Holy Spirit: "Set apart for me Barnabas and Saul for the work to which I have called them" (Acts 13:2). We are not told how the Holy Spirit communicated this message to the leaders, but it became clear to all that Barnabas and Saul were God's choice. This would be an excellent pattern for every pulpit committee and search committee to follow: "worshiping the Lord and fasting."

In an earlier chapter, I mentioned how prayer became a great source of encouragement to me. It also became a channel through which I gained discernment. The Lord never appeared to me in a dream or with any special effects, but He made His guidance very clear to me as I continually sought Him in prayer.

After my resignation from the church in Minnesota, nearly twenty-five inquiries came across my desk. At first there was just a slight trickle, but as the weeks passed, the pace increased and so did the uneasiness. No longer did I have the benefit of choosing between two or three options. The options increased and I became more confused. So I took the matter before the Lord.

As I sought His counsel, the thought entered my mind to identify as clearly and specifically as possible my personal strengths and weaknesses. I listed all the possible attributes I was looking for in a new ministry and those that would complement my strengths. Then I wrote down where

I was in my life—rapidly approaching the half-century mark—and what ministry I could invest the next fifteen to twenty years in.

I continued to pray for clarity of thought. Once everything was on paper, I could see the type of ministry I would prefer, where I would be able to experience a wonderful, equal yoke. This process narrowed the opportunities to two, and eventually I chose the one where I am now serving the Lord.

One of the greatest problems we face when praying about a decision is that we are inclined to ask for God's approval of a decision we've already made, upon which we have not yet taken any action. Like the young woman who informs her parents, "Mom and Dad, this is Bill. We've known each other for several weeks and are madly in love. I know this may come as a shock, but we've decided to get married. I'm sure you'll come to like him as much as I do. Just give it some time. We would like your blessing on our marriage. Will you give it?" That's a lot different than asking Mom and Dad for guidance concerning a potential marriage. Likewise, when we seek God's direction in prayer, we must ask for His wisdom, not His approval for a predetermined decision.

DISCERN WITH COMMON SENSE

It is possible for prayer and Scripture to become a "cop out" for decision making. How often I've heard someone say, "But I prayed about it, so it has to be the right decision," or, "I claimed this promise from God's Word, so I know this is what He wants me to do." Prayer and Bible reading are excellent checkpoints, but they should not be used in isolation from other sound guidelines. For instance, the Lord has also provided each believer with common sense. It makes good sense not to remarry soon after the loss of a spouse. Emotions have not yet settled and one may choose to marry for all the wrong reasons. Common sense will also tell you not to go into any partnership when obvious disagreements already exist or where the partners hardly know one another.

When I was contemplating a new ministry, common sense dictated that I inquire whether any of the present staff had a desire and a following to become the senior pastor of the church. Common sense encouraged me to check out the debt load the church was carrying in relationship to the faithfulness of the members to deal with debt. Common sense motivated me to take the spiritual and political temperature of the congregation. It didn't take a lot of profound insight to come up with those inquiries and insights—just some common sense.

This was apparently the checkpoint used by the church at Jerusalem during a doctrinal dispute. The apostles and elders met to investigate some allegations against a number of believing Pharisees who were reported to be teaching that "the Gentiles must be circumcised and required to obey the law of Moses" (Acts 15:5). The allegations were correct, and the teaching was wrong.

Therefore, after much debate on the issue, here was their conclusion: "It seemed good to the Holy Spirit and to us not to burden you with anything beyond the following requirements: You are to abstain from food sacrificed to idols, from blood, from the meat of strangled animals and from sexual immorality. You will do well to avoid these things" (Acts 15:28-29). Earlier in the passage when James spoke, he drew upon the wisdom from Scripture and the men who spoke, concluding with this common-sense approach, "It is my judgment, therefore, that we should not make it difficult for the Gentiles who are turning to God"

(Acts 15:19). Consider what you've experienced in the past and what you know from Scripture and then draw upon common sense. But even then you are still not ready for a final decision.

DISCERN WITH WISE COUNSEL
AND AFFIRMATION FROM OTHERS

Another source of wisdom is other people. I sought wise counsel from many friends. Everyone I conversed with agreed on the type of church I should seek, as well as the strengths and weaknesses they saw in me. When I narrowed the choice to two possibilities, my friends once again confirmed that choice.

After we moved to Orange and began to minister in the church, we had dozens of visitors from our former church in Minnesota. All who came agreed the church was exactly as I had previously described it and became excited when they envisioned what the Lord might do in this ministry.

I believe this was the approach the apostle Paul took when he had to make a decision about where he should preach the gospel next. The doors were closed for him in Asia and Bithynia (Acts 16:6-7). Paul and his companions then traveled to the city of Troas, where the apostle had a night vision. He saw a Macedonian standing and begging him, "Come over to Macedonia and help us" (Acts 16:9).

Notice the next step: "After Paul had seen the vision, we got ready at once to leave for Macedonia, concluding that God had called us to preach the gospel to them" (Acts 16:10). Who did the "concluding"? This was not Paul's decision alone. He shared the vision with his colleagues. They affirmed that what he had seen was from the Lord and interpreted the vision as a call to Macedonia.

Allow me to make two specific suggestions as you consult friends. Be careful not to seek out those who will tell you what they think you want to hear because they don't want to hurt your feelings or to jeopardize your friendship. Second, don't ignore advice from concerned friends simply because their counsel does not support your desires or interests.

Many years ago, a young king ascended the throne and was immediately confronted by some concerned citizens of the kingdom. They implored, "Your father put a heavy yoke on us, but now lighten the harsh labor and the heavy yoke he put on us, and we will serve you" (2 Chronicles 10:4). Not knowing what action to take, he first consulted the elders, who had served his father. They advised, "If you will be kind to these people and please them and give them a favorable answer, they will always be your servants" (2 Chronicles 10:7). That advice struck a nerve in the young king's life. Youth enjoys a challenge. To give in to those people would have been a blow to the king's ego. He thought, "What can one expect from a group of old men who are too weak to fight and too fearful of putting discontents in their place. I'll go to my real friends with whom I grew up and see what they say."

King Rehoboam rejected the counsel of the elders and consulted his cronies. The young advisers instructed, "Tell the people who have said to you, 'Your father put a heavy yoke on us, but make our yoke lighter'—tell them, 'My little finger is thicker than my father's waist. My father laid on you a heavy yoke; I will make it even heavier. My father scourged you with whips; I will scourge you with scorpions'" (2 Chronicles 10:10-11). This is what King Rehoboam wanted to hear all along. This would save face and show the people that he was a king to be feared and obeyed. But he should have listened to the elders, because by following the advice of his young friends, Rehoboam lost more than eighty-five percent of his kingdom.

What qualities should one look for in the people from whom he seeks counsel? Those individuals should (1) have your best interests at heart; (2) show evidence of spiritual maturity; (3) have made good decisions themselves; (4) be objective and not emotionally involved; and (5) tell you what they feel you need to hear, not necessarily what you want to hear.

DISCERN BY OBSERVING NEEDS AND OPPORTUNITIES

You've heard it said before: "Some people see an opportunity and ask, 'Why?' Others look at it and ask, 'Why not?'" So many people walk through life in a fog, wondering what they should do with their lives. Yet needs and opportunities cry out for attention all around them. Jesus said it well when He told His disciples, "Do you not say, 'Four months more and then the harvest'? I tell you, open your eyes and look at the fields! They are ripe for harvest" (John 4:35). Too often we walk around as though blind. We ask, "God, what do you want me to do?" His response would be, "Open your eyes and see the hurts and suffering, the confusion and chaos, the injustice and immorality, the spiritual bankruptcy of your neighbors, colleagues at work, and friends. Do something to meet these needs."

Our sons are preparing for professional ministry today because a youth director took them to Mexicali, Mexico, for several visits during three consecutive spring vacations. They observed both physical and spiritual poverty, had opportunities to play with the children and teenagers in the village, and shared their testimonies with groups and individuals. They made friends with those who could not speak their language. In the process, both sons captured a vision for ministry and a desire to invest the rest of their lives in full-time service for Jesus Christ.

Some of our friends in Minnesota have a cabin in Wisconsin. Since summer is a time when many people go to their lake cabins, Dave and Jinny decided to use the weekends to begin an outreach ministry in their area. Throughout the entire summer, they held services in their cabin and reached between twenty and forty cabin owners, many of whom did not know the Lord. Their ability to see a need and meet it has paid great spiritual dividends, both for them and their friends.

At times our minds dwell so much on the necessities of life, such as what to eat, what to wear, or where to live, that we don't see the needs and opportunities in our midst. Much good in life has been accomplished simply because someone who has gone through a difficult time has opened his eyes and observed others who also hurt. So he developed a ministry or a means of helping the hurting.

What need do you see that has not yet been met? What opportunity looms before you and challenges you to capture it? Look around and seize the opportunities in which others have little or no interest.

DISCERN BY EVALUATING
THE DESIRES OF YOUR HEART

Let me say at the outset that this principle is very subjective. And one of the problems you'll face is deciding whether your desires correspond with God's desires. It's so easy to fool ourselves and spiritualize our wishes so that they seem God-honoring. We've all read about the end result of desires gone astray during the 1987 "holy war" among the TV evangelists, including sex and financial scandal.

So how do we determine which desires are ego gratification and which come from the Lord? First, it is important to know that God does place desires in our hearts. The Bible states, "It is God who works in you to will and to act according to his good purpose" (Philippians 2:13). The Lord gives us the will to do what is good. Whenever I choose to do something that is good, I can thank God for placing that desire in my heart. On the other hand, when I desire what is not good for me or for others, I can attribute it to myself.

A second principle to consider is that each of my desires needs to be evaluated in terms of what God has already revealed to me in Scripture. If I desire to take another man's wife, I can be certain that such a desire was not planted in my heart by God, for He already revealed that such an act is wrong when He wrote on the tablets, "You shall not covet your neighbor's house. You shall not covet your neighbor's wife, or his manservant or maidservant, his ox or donkey, or anything that belongs to your neighbor" (Exodus 20:17).

On the other hand, if I desire to help someone who is hurting, to encourage the discouraged, or to impart God's truth to one who has not heard or has not understood, I can conclude that God has placed those good desires in my heart.

A third way of evaluating the source of your desires is to determine your relationship with the Lord. The more time you spend with Him, the more you will want what He wants for you. That's why the psalmist David was able to say, "Delight yourself in the LORD and he will give you the desires of your heart" (Psalm 37:4). Again he writes, "May he give you the desire of your heart and make all your plans succeed" (Psalm 20:4).

Since I graduated from seminary back in 1964, I've had a desire to live in Southern California. At that time, we had a possible opportunity to work in a church in Santa Ana, California. But the door closed on that possibility and we moved north to Minneapolis instead. Now, after twenty-three years, we live in Orange, a neighboring city to Santa Ana. Was that desire from the Lord or just from me? I believe God may have originally placed the desire within me many years ago, but I was not yet prepared to have it fulfilled.

When I told the Lord that I'd go wherever He wanted me to go, the Lord recognized this availability as my true desire. That commitment took me from Dallas to Minneapolis; to Winnipeg, Canada; to Fresno, California; back to Minneapolis; and finally out to Orange, California. In all truthfulness, the Lord has given me the desire of my heart in each move I made. It's just that this time His plan coincided with an earlier desire I possessed.

What do you really want from the Lord today? Is it in agreement or in conflict with what God has already revealed in His Word? Are you walking closely with Him or do you find that your relationship is a hit-or-miss situation? As you answer these questions, you'll be better able to discern the origin of your desires.

Thus far we have looked at eight principles for discerning while you wait on the Lord. They include discerning with Scripture, prayer, common sense, wise counsel, and affirmation from others; observing needs and opportunities; and evaluating the desires of your heart. Let's consider one more way to discern: time.

DISCERN WITH TIME

Time may seem like a terrible enemy as it passes so slowly without any definitive results. You look for changes, but they don't appear. You relish the day when everything will come to an end as you leave God's waiting room, but in spite of the passing of time, you remain where you are and wait.

But I have found time itself to be a source of *healing and clarifying*. You may not realize it as much when you are in the thick of the battle, but your emotions are being frayed. You may wake up one day and find yourself crying for no apparent reason. You may notice yourself getting so tired that you don't even want to get out of bed the next day. Everything starts to bother you, especially small, inconsequential events. You need time to heal. Time to renew your strength. Time to get in the Word and gain a new perspective on life.

With a renewed perspective, time will no longer be your enemy, but will become a very dear friend. I savored those days and weeks in transition. I used the time to jog, to write, to visit places I hadn't been before, to attend other churches and learn all I could about worship, to think, to talk with friends, to socialize, and to plan for the future. All this provided the opportunity to heal physically and emotionally.

You may have experienced the loss of a spouse or family member. Perhaps you've experienced the trauma of divorce, or have walked into work one day and were told, "We won't be needing your services anymore." Maybe you've had your fill of rejection or have gone through the nightmare of child or wife abuse. You need time to heal. If the experience has been fairly recent, you are probably too close to the situation to make a wise decision on the next steps to take. Allow yourself time to heal emotionally, mentally, physically, and spiritually.

A second benefit of time is that it helps you clarify your thinking. When we lived in Fresno, I never looked forward to traveling during the months of January through March, especially if I had to fly. The San Joaquin Valley becomes enshrouded in a low, thick fog that may hang in the valley for days. Sometimes it burns off by ten o'clock in the morning. At other times the airport is closed down. Sometimes I've spent many hours waiting for the fog to lift, only to return to my home, hoping for better weather the next morning. The determining factor to decide whether the plane should take off is if one can look across the runway and see the control tower. Once it is visible, you can prepare to board.

When you are in the midst of the battle, it's difficult to see what decision is best. You need time to allow the fog of the hour to dissipate so that you can see the issues clearly enough to make a wise decision.

Within months of leaving the church in Minnesota, I wrote a manuscript that drew heavily from the experiences I encountered there. I asked a number of my friends to read it. I received similar replies from most people: "You have a little too much detail, and some places come across a little judgmentally. You may want to back off a little and rework the manuscript." They were absolutely right. I put the manuscript away and have not touched it in a year. When I finish writing this book, I plan to carefully read through that manuscript once again and either rework what I've written or scrap it altogether. I still have not decided whether I'll even try to get it published. It has served as an excellent journal, but now with the passing of time, I see things differently. I've been able to observe the Lord at work in the life of the church, the lives of some of those opposed to my remaining as senior pastor, and my own personal life. In the entire process, I have had the privilege of seeing God's Word verified time and again.

As you look at the options that lie before you, allow yourself enough time to heal and to see things more clearly. Your decisions will be better when you are willing to wait.

Today you may be ready to make some life-changing decisions. Before you do, consider those pilots who sit in the cockpit and go through a long checklist. Then look at the checklist of this chapter: (1) discern with Scripture; (2) discern with prayer; (3) discern with common sense; (4) discern with wise counsel; (5) discern by observing needs and opportunities; (6) evaluate the desires of your heart; and (7) allow time to pass. Don't make hasty, emotional decisions as you wait for God to work in the circumstances of your life. Allow Him to remain in control and to complete in you what He has already started. Then seek Him with all your heart as you begin to decide your future. He has promised, "Trust in the LORD with all your heart and lean not on your own understanding; in all your ways acknowledge him, and he will make your paths straight. Do not be wise in your own eyes; fear the LORD and shun evil. This will bring health to your body and nourishment to your bones" (Proverbs 3:5-8).

10

The Viewing Room

It was March of 1957. I stood at my mother's casket in a viewing room, observing the body she had abandoned when she entered into the presence of her Lord. As I now reflect on that experience, I recall some of the feelings I encountered and some specific characteristics indicative of a room for viewing the deceased.

VIEWING ROOM ATTRIBUTES

The first reflection that surfaces to my attention is the fact that the body of a loved one lies at rest in a casket. The mortician takes pains to make the corpse look natural—as though the deceased is asleep. When I looked at Mother's body lying peacefully in the new pink dress she had worn a year earlier at my sister's wedding, she looked as though she were merely sleeping. At times I found myself expecting her to awaken shortly.

Second, a line of friends and acquaintances stood in the room to offer words of encouragement and condolence, as they greeted our family and then passed by the casket to view the body that Mother vacated. Some forced smiles, attempting to be positive in the midst of the great loss, but we knew that their hearts, along with ours, were consumed with grief. When the battle for life is long and painful, relatives and friends experience a mixture of anguish and peace—anguish because the battle has been lost, but peace because they know that God has declared His will by taking this loved one to be with Him. On the other hand, when death has been unexpected and quick, as in the case of Mother, feelings usually consist of numbness and unbelief.

Furthermore, the future looks bleak when you are in the viewing room. The closest survivors to the deceased are often so consumed with the sense of loss that they have little time to consider life without their loved one. In my grief, I strained to consider what the future might hold, but I was aware that Dad's mind was focused more on the present than the future because of the responsibilities of making funeral arrangements, answering phone calls, and responding to visiting relatives, neighbors, and friends.

Then there are those precious memories of the departed person that drift in and out of one's mind. I thought about the better days: the fun times, the jokes, and funny things Mom said and did; the warm times, the intimate times, the conversations. All those past memories flooded my mind as I stood beside Mother's casket.

My mind was also interrupted with thoughts of what might have been if Mother had survived, if she had remained in good health: the places Dad and Mom could have gone together, the projects they could have worked on together, the fun times they would have had. But the plans would now have to be scrapped. One of the places Mother had always wanted to visit was California. Maybe that's where the seed desire was planted in my own heart.

I can remember thinking, "Why would the Lord not allow her to have that experience she had looked forward to for so many years?" Then I began to laugh when I realized how earthly my thoughts were. To imagine that I was feeling sorry for Mother because she never got to go to California but had to go to heaven instead! Now that I live in California, I have little question that she got the better deal.

A sixth reflection that surfaces to my mind is my remembrance of some feelings of guilt: those thoughts and feelings of "I should have said this or that" or "I should have done thus and so." I thought about those lost opportunities when I might have encouraged Mom, thanked her, or just told her how much I loved her. I caught myself saying some things to Mom while in the viewing room, but I knew those words were falling on ears that could no longer hear.

I also remember feeling guilty for some things I said over the years, and for the times when I was too busy to write or call when I was at school in Philadelphia. I felt guilty about the times when I would come home on the weekends, say hello, eat a meal, and immediately take off to see my girlfriend. How I would love to spend some time talking to Mother now.

I also remember the fragrance and beauty of the flowers that adorned the viewing room: expressions of love, as well as an attempt to make something as ugly as death seem somewhat pleasant. I've discovered over the years that death in the Bible is never viewed as something of beauty. Death is like a thief that steals our dearest possessions: a child, a husband or wife, a mother or father, or a friend. Death took someone I loved. I wondered whether life could ever have meaning without Mom being around.

ANOTHER TYPE OF VIEWING ROOM

What does my experience thirty years ago have to do with God's waiting room today? I see many parallels between the two experiences. Sometimes the waiting room leads to the viewing room. No matter what the doctor does for the patient, he or she dies. The person may have been young or old, sick or healthy. But a time comes when, through an accident, illness, or an unexpected breakdown of a bodily organ, a person enters the death process, and every attempt to revive the patient fails.

Mother was only forty-four years old. She would have been seventy-four today. According to the insurance charts, she should still be alive. But life was cut short. No amount of effort brought her back to life once the aorta in her heart ruptured. So we were forced to make the passage from a waiting room experience of several days to the viewing room.

My experience at the Minneapolis church was also short-lived. I spent only two years in that ministry. The life span of ministry in my previous church had been thirteen years, so my departure from Minneapolis seemed premature. However, when the patient (my ministry) became sick and the heart was weak, I did not have the skills to make it survive. No matter what I did, I could not bring the ministry back to life. And so the ministry, under my leadership, died. And I moved from the waiting room into the viewing room.

At that point, all the thoughts and feelings I had experienced in that 1957 viewing room surfaced once again. The grief, the numbness, the sense of loss, and the guilt returned. My wife and I stood in line at our "farewell" while our friends passed by with their words of condolence and encouragement.

As I stood in the reception line to greet my friends, I

could not help but reflect on the good times, the fun times, the jokes, and the good relationships we had built. Thoughts of what might have been flashed through my mind, while questions about the future were blocked out by the immediacy of the hour. I knew that death had once again crept into my life and removed something else I dearly loved, only this time the deceased was the opportunity to minister among people I had grown to love and appreciate. Again, death was no friend. I would have to prepare once more for a transition.

As you read these pages, you too may have recently entered a viewing room. Perhaps as you have waited upon the Lord, you have hoped that He would somehow change the circumstances in a favorable way. You have prayed that the patient would not die, but death has become a reality. Your patient may be a person, an opportunity, a job, a dream, a ministry, an ambition, an unrealized goal, a business, an education, a change of heart, or the direction of a loved one. But instead of life, you see only death. The battle has been lost. It's over. So where do you go from here? The next step is to make a trip to the burial site.

AFTER THE VIEWING ROOM

The burial site is the place of ultimate finality. As the casket is lowered into the ground, you become painfully aware that it is the last time you will have any visual contact with the deceased until the Lord returns or until you also die. Once the graveside ceremony has been completed, you either return to the church or to a home where a meal is prepared for very special guests and friends.

In my case, my resignation was not the final step. There were individuals and groups who talked about returning their senior pastor to the pulpit. I was not in a position to either desire or think about a reversal of my decision. Convinced that the Lord had closed this particular chapter of my life, I had no plans to reconsider. Finality was still not a reality, even after my last message Sunday evening. Nor did it hit home during the viewing room experience as we said our goodbyes to those very special people in the congregation.

I guess the burial site experience occurred when we returned home after the farewell reception. Only a few of us remained in the church fellowship hall, and then we got into our car and drove home. That's when the reality of a deceased ministry hit me. It was finished. There was no turning back. The goodbyes had been said. The hugs had been given. The words of condolence and encouragement had been spoken. There was nothing more to do at this point but to leave the church premises and begin thinking about where we would go from there.

And yet there was one more step in this scenario: an opportunity to be with our closest friends, whom we had known for many years, and others who had become very intimate friends in the midst of the deepest waters. So we left the church and went to a restaurant with some friends, where we kept the conversation light and humorous. That was the fellowship after the burial, which provided the finality we needed.

Maybe you are still holding on to some hope that your situation will still turn around. Don't lose sight of that possibility until God makes it very clear that the patient has died. Don't pull the plug prematurely. But if the time comes when all who know and love you agree that the battle is over, accept the facts, bury the body, stay close to your friends, and prepare for the new challenges that lie before you. That next phase of your life will be your transition into a new chapter.

THE TRANSITIONAL OR ADJUSTMENT PHASE

Now what are you going to do with the rest of your life? That question is almost impossible to ask when you are in the viewing room or at the burial site. But the time comes when you must say with the apostle Paul, "Forgetting what is behind and straining toward what is ahead, I press on toward the goal to win the prize for which God has called me heavenward in Christ Jesus" (Philippians 3:13-14).

You may have thought that the waiting room experience was very difficult and the viewing room was almost unbearable. Don't expect that the transitional time will be a bowl of cherries. It too has its pitfalls and setbacks, but it can also be a period of wonderful excitement and anticipation. You will probably be making some adjustments: physical, emotional, mental, spiritual, and maybe even geographical or occupational. For instance, when you go through a period of prolonged stress, your body is affected adversely. You could experience headaches, backaches, rapid heartbeats, weight gain or loss, ulcers, stomach upsets, high blood pressure, change in sleeping habits, and physical exhaustion.

I have already mentioned how my body was affected several years ago when I experienced prolonged stress. My heart began to beat rapidly at times. I had a difficult time sleeping because I could hear my heartbeat no matter which direction I turned my head on the pillow. I understood clearly what David meant when he cried to the Lord, "My heart pounds, my strength fails me; even the light has gone from my eyes" (Psalm 38:10). Fortunately, during my stressful experience in Minneapolis, I noticed few adverse physical effects other than a weariness and a gain of weight because I was spending so much time with friends at breakfast, lunch, dinner, and evening snacks. So finally I determined to make the necessary adjustments.

First, I dealt with my weariness problem by getting away from Minneapolis for about ten days and going back to my family in Pennsylvania. During that period I was able to get a lot of rest, think things through more clearly, and initiate a jogging program.

Another transitional problem I faced was the drain on my emotional stability. Up to about the last month throughout my two-year ordeal, I felt quite stable emotionally. In spite of the discouragements, the setbacks and criticisms, my spirits remained high and positive. Many in the congregation confided that they marveled at how well I was handling the pressures. I told them that my sustaining power came from the Lord and their prayers. What a confidence-builder to know that so many people were praying, sending letters of encouragement, and giving verbal support!

But eventually my emotional batteries had discharged to the point of depletion. My spirit was broken and I had nothing left with which to "fight back." Once I was convinced that I had exhausted all my resources, it was time to close shop and see what the Lord had in mind from that point on. I had little difficulty identifying with David, who wrote, "I am worn out from groaning; all night long I flood my bed with weeping and drench my couch with tears. My eyes grow weak with sorrow; they fail because of all my foes" (Psalm 6:6-7). "Save me, O God, for the waters have come up to my neck. I sink in the miry depths, where there is no foothold. I have come into the deep waters; the floods engulf me. I am worn out calling for help; my throat is parched. My eyes fail, looking for my God" (Psalm 69:1-3).

My emotional batteries were recharged slowly during my seven-month transition by various means. Probably the greatest help came by getting away from the source of my stress: the ministry in that specific church. Some friends invited us to their cabin several times during the summer months. And in the early fall I had several speaking engagements in Illinois, California, and Texas. After my week-long ministry in Dallas, my wife and I headed to Florida for some rest and relaxation, thanks to some Minneapolis friends, and then made our way up the East Coast to Pennsylvania, where we spent about a month. During that time I wrote one of my manuscripts, which kept me busy and productive. Also, the subject of my manuscript provided an emotional catharsis.

The testing of my emotional stability surfaced when I was asked to return to my former church and participate in an ordination service for one of my former staff members, a personal friend whom I had known for eighteen years. I hesitated when he first asked, but because of our longstanding friendship, I agreed to speak. By the grace of God, I had no negative emotional response, and I felt that it was the best thing I could have done to verify the sustaining power of the Lord.

I realize that not everyone can get away from his source of stress. But when there has been a great loss and you have spent time in the viewing room, it is important to do everything in your power to leave the place where the stress was so great. For someone who has lost a spouse, the surviving partner may sell the house and move to another location. It offers a sense of a new beginning. Other individuals will take a long vacation, or visit friends or relatives in another city.

Another transition that I needed to confront was my mental condition, my thought process. Since I had accumulated a lot of questions in God's waiting room and then added to the stack of unanswered issues while in the viewing room, I needed to take time to think, and in some cases rethink, what I believed.

When I felt that I had lost the battle, my self-confidence was at an all-time low. I questioned my ability to preach, my effectiveness as a leader, and my fitness to be a pastor. After all, I had never experienced a major failure before in my life. Now what was I to do with all these unanswered questions?

As I spent time in the Scriptures, I was reminded not to evaluate my ability solely on the basis of how people responded to my ministry. I discovered afresh that all the prophets and apostles experienced rejection, both of their message and of themselves. In fact, the apostle Paul spent an entire chapter (1 Corinthians 9) defending his right to be supported by the believers in Corinth. But many of them preferred Peter and Apollos over Paul. They compared one apostle with another. Each group had its favorite (1 Corinthians 1:10-12, 3:4-7). Some felt that Paul was a poor speaker, that he was not as eloquent as Apollos (1 Corinthians 2:1-5, Acts 18:24-28).

So I had to recognize that there will always be those who will not like my style of preaching or teaching. Nor will everyone respond to my form of leadership. But I concluded that people's responses did not determine the gifts God had given me. So I had to rethink how God had equipped me, accept what He had given me, and use it to the best of my ability, leaving the results up to God.

Perhaps you have just gone through a divorce or have been turned down for a job and feel terribly rejected. Your self-image has been crushed. You've begun to think that no one loves you or that you can no longer trust anyone. You're starting to question whether you have anything to offer anyone. You already feel like a second-class citizen. That is certainly not the case. But you will have to reevaluate who you are in the eyes of the Lord. How has He equipped you to function? Don't look at yourself in light of the problem you've experienced or what a friend or spouse has said about you. What does God say about you? He thinks you are someone special and He isn't finished with you. He still has plans for you. You *do* have a future!

The fourth transition adjustment was my spiritual life. During the waiting room experience, I spent my first hour of each day in the Word and in prayer, a practice I continue to this day. They were precious times, filled with a lot of encouragement from Scripture and many requests for strength, wisdom, and love for others. But in my transitional period, I found myself spending more time in praise and thanksgiving and less in asking. I desired to worship the Lord in my private time more than request that He do things for me. I still needed a church to pastor and a lot of healing to take place, but my focus was on praise and worship.

I began to go through the alphabet, listing attributes of God with each letter. For instance, A=almighty, B=beauty, C=concern/compassion, D=dominance, E=everlasting/eternal/exalted, F=forgiving, etc. Then as I worshiped God, I praised Him for each quality and elaborated on each in my time of prayer. This resulted in a much greater optimism for the future and deeper appreciation of God.

Another spiritual adjustment dealt with my tongue. I knew I would be tempted to talk about the past and focus on those who were in opposition to me, so I continually brought this matter to the Lord and prayed with the psalmist David, "Set a guard over my mouth, O LORD; keep watch over the door of my lips" (Psalm 141:3). "May the words of my mouth and the meditation of my heart be pleasing in your sight, O LORD, my Rock and my Redeemer" (Psalm 19:14). I was never one hundred percent successful, but I made good progress and got to the point where I was able to turn negative conversations to a more positive direction.

The third spiritual adjustment was to observe God's faithfulness as never before. I continue to marvel how the Lord provided for so many of the concerns I had before I made my decision to resign. I became very security-conscious, which surprised me because I had never been that way before. But since I was about to turn fifty, with two sons in college and medical bills that I was not certain would be picked up by the insurance company, it became a little disconcerting. I also wrestled with the thought of moving to another geographical location. I wondered, "Will we be able to afford housing? Will our health insurance continue once we've left the church? What kind of a ministry will match my gifts and style of leadership?"

The Lord graciously dealt with each of these issues, one at a time. He not only met our financial needs, health insurance needs, occupational needs, and housing needs, but He also provided a ministry that matched my gifts and leadership abilities beautifully.

Your spiritual life may have received a powerful blow. Perhaps you've been forced to rethink what you really believe about God and His way of operating in your life. Maybe you need to deal with hostile feelings that originate in an unforgiving heart. Or it could be an area of pride that needs to be addressed and removed. Whatever your spiritual need at this moment, God is sufficient to help you in your transition.

The one other area of adjustment in my experience was my tendency to compare the present with the past. Sometimes I felt like the old men who attended the dedication of the Temple foundation after it had been laid:

> All the people gave a great shout of praise to the
> LORD, because the foundation of the house of the
> LORD was laid. But many of the older priests and

Levites and family heads, who had seen the former temple, wept aloud when they saw the foundation of this temple being laid, while many others shouted for joy. No one could distinguish the sound of the shouts of joy from the sound of weeping, because the people made so much noise. And the sound was heard far away. (Ezra 3:11-13)

Why were the old men weeping? The answer is given in the book of Haggai: "Who of you is left who saw this house in its former glory? How does it look to you now? Does it not seem to you like nothing? But now be strong . . ." (Haggai 2:3-4). Also, in the book of Zechariah, God challenged the people, "The hands of Zerubbabel have laid the foundation of this temple; his hands will also complete it. Then you will know that the LORD Almighty has sent me to you. Who despises the day of small things? Men will rejoice when they see the plumb line in the hand of Zerubbabel" (Zechariah 4:9-10).

The old men were comparing the present with the past and didn't like what they saw. They remembered the splendor and vastness of Solomon's Temple. It was enriched with gold and intricately carved woodwork. Solomon's Temple was awesome. But the new Temple seemed less ornate, not as ambitious an undertaking—almost second-rate.

Most of us have difficulty trying to imagine life after the viewing room. We convince ourselves that nothing could ever be as good as it once was. We think that life won't have much meaning without the position, the job, the friend, or the relative we have lost.

I cannot help but think of a young man who was a member of another Minneapolis congregation. As he was playing baseball early one evening, he slid into home plate and didn't get up. I don't know if anyone understands exactly what happened, but something stopped functioning in his body and today he is a quadriplegic. First came the initial shock that his life as he had known it was now gone. It would never return. And as he looked out into the future, everything seemed quite bleak. His greatest moments of discouragement came when his mind drifted back to the good old days, which were only a year or so ago. His transition has been long and painful, but he will eventually succeed in that transition and will experience a meaningful but different future.

Once you've gone from the waiting room into the viewing room, out to the burial site and then into the transitional stage, you are then prepared to enter the new-life phase.

THE NEW-LIFE PHASE

As one enters this dimension of life he begins to get a settled feeling. He feels more comfortable with his new surroundings, whether that includes new friends, location, or job. The flashbacks to the past become more infrequent. One's thoughts and energy are directed toward the present and the future. Many ties with the past have been broken, though some residual effects will be carried into the present.

When we left our former ministry, we sensed God leading us out of one situation into something new. Therefore, we left with dignity and a deeply rooted love for the majority of people in the church. I determined to leave with the attitude that I could return for a visit with a clear conscience, a pure heart, and enough love to hug everyone who was willing to welcome me back.

We have been able to keep in touch with our past

through phone calls, visits from many members in our former church, letters, and the church newsletter. We've maintained a continued interest in what God is doing in the lives of our friends and the church, so we asked to remain on the mailing list.

Then one year after my resignation, we returned to Minneapolis to attend our Free Church National Convention. I contacted the new pastor and had breakfast with him so that I could get to know and encourage him in the task at hand. I also felt that before I visited the secretaries and staff at the church, I should ask his permission and not do anything that might jeopardize his ministry at the church. He graciously granted the permission and encouraged me to visit whenever I was in town.

The next item on my agenda was to renew friendships and acquaintances among the secretarial and ministerial staff. I committed myself to remain positive, to say nothing negative about anyone or anything, and to show my support for the new pastor.

I likened this visit to the few times when I've gone to the grave site of my mother. I know she is no longer at the spot where her marker is located, but rather she is enjoying precious times with her Lord. In a similar manner, when I returned to Minneapolis and visited my former church, I experienced no sense of it being my ministry. Those days are gone. Some of the effects remain, but the ministry itself has now gone to Orange.

Your own past may flash through your mind at different times as you recall the life that existed before you ever imagined there could be a viewing room experience for you. But as time passes, those memories are not quite as painful or even as frequent. You start thinking more about what you are doing today and what you may be doing in the future.

LESSONS FROM THE VIEWING ROOM

As I look back on my viewing room experience, I recognize two helpful lessons. First, I've made the commitment to incorporate into my life everything I've learned through my experience. I don't want to relearn the lessons the Lord has taught me through the difficulties. For instance, one of the changes I made as a college student after my mother's death was to start taking pictures of those I love. Why? Because I had so few pictures of Mother. So I asked for a 35mm camera for Christmas and began a new hobby of photography. I've shot and developed hundreds of rolls of film over the years. I've taken slides, color prints, polaroid pictures, 8mm movies, super 8mm movies, and video. When people see me coming, they duck because they expect a camera to pop out from somewhere and catch them as they are. I have made numerous changes in my life because of what God has taught me during the past few years.

A second lesson that encouraged me was that God blesses those who place their confidence in Him. So I anticipated that the next chapter of my life would be fruitful. I don't say that because I feel I deserve His blessing, but rather because I have followed God's Word to the best of my ability and know that whatever a man sows, he will also reap. My desire has been to sow integrity, dignity, and love in my relationships with people. When you do that, you cannot help but reap a lot of love and support from people.

I believe that my present ministry will be effective because of what God did in the recent past. He smoothed out some rough edges, filled in some cavities, and is gradually shaping me into what He wants me to become.

The viewing room is excruciatingly painful. But the day will come when you step out of that room, bury the past, make your transition, and begin your new life.

11
The Benefits of Waiting

Most people do not enjoy waiting, whether in line at the supermarket, in traffic jams, or in the doctor's office. And waiting for someone to show up for an appointment can be very exasperating. Though many agree that patience is a virtue, few can wait to be patient.

We live in an instant-gratification society. Few people wait until marriage to experience intimate sexual relations. Others plunge into financial debt because they can't wait until they can afford what they want. And some people make very unwise decisions because they did not wait long enough to check out all the facts.

And when God invites us to pause in His waiting room, we just about flip out and cry for immediate deliverance. Why? Because we see only the painful process of waiting, but fail to understand its benefits.

Some people would understandably question, "How could waiting possibly provide any benefit? The only thing I ever get is frustration." I've wrestled with the same question in my mind. "Is there truly any advantage to waiting upon the Lord?" Yes there is, and I would like to relate to you some of the gains you may receive as you wait.

WAITING ALLOWS GOD THE TIME TO COMPLETE HIS WORK IN YOU

The apostle Paul informed his readers in Philippi that he was "confident of this, that he who began a good work in you will carry it on to completion until the day of Christ Jesus" (Philippians 1:6). God's plan in your life does not include shortcuts. Like a good spaghetti sauce that needs time to simmer and mature in flavor, so we need to be placed on the back burner at different times in life so that the Lord can continue the process He started years ago.

God is a Master Craftsman. And it always takes time to craft quality, which is what God is doing in your life. He is perfecting, developing, and smoothing out the rough edges in every life. Observe how God crafted some of His special people in biblical days.

GOD CRAFTED HUMILITY IN MOSES AND NEBUCHADNEZZAR

Though Moses committed murder in his early years and possessed so little knowledge of God that he needed to ask God His name, this man passed through God's refining process, and later became known as "a very humble man, more humble than anyone else on the face of the earth" (Numbers 12:3).

Humility does not develop overnight. Man's natural quality is pride, so God has to take us through the process of hard times until we recognize who He is and who we are. An ancient king of Babylon named Nebuchadnezzar experienced such a process. He was forewarned by the prophet Daniel that unless he repented of his sins and acknowledged the Most High as sovereign over all the kingdoms of men, he would experience a seven-year waiting room, be driven from his kingdom, and live like a madman. The king rejected Daniel's warning and continued to do what he pleased.

One night Nebuchadnezzar was out on the roof of his palace, perusing his kingdom and saying to himself, "Is not this the great Babylon I have built as the royal residence, by my mighty power and for the glory of my majesty?" (Daniel 4:30). While the words were still on his lips, a voice from heaven informed him that his royal authority had been removed and that he would live like an animal for seven years until he acknowledged that the Most High was sovereign over the kingdoms of men, giving them to anyone He desired.

At that point, Nebuchadnezzar began to experience the life of a recluse, driven away from people, eating grass like cattle, with his hair looking like the feathers of an eagle and his nails like the claws of a bird. His testimony concerning what had happened after that seven-year waiting experience is recorded for all posterity to read and learn from:

> At the end of that time, I, Nebuchadnezzar, raised my eyes toward heaven, and my sanity was restored. Then I praised the Most High; I honored and glorified him who lives forever. His dominion is an eternal dominion; his kingdom endures from generation to generation. All the peoples of the earth are regarded as nothing. He does as he pleases with the powers of heaven and the peoples of the earth. No one can hold back his hand or say to him: "What

have you done?" At the same time that my sanity was restored, my honor and splendor were returned to me for the glory of my kingdom. My advisers and nobles sought me out, and I was restored to my throne and became even greater than before. Now I, Nebuchadnezzar, praise and exalt and glorify the King of heaven, because everything he does is right and all his ways are just. And those who walk in pride he is able to humble. (Daniel 4:34-37)

The king left God's waiting room only after he acknowledged it was the Lord and not himself who was in charge of life. When he was willing to give God the honor due Him and recognize that all he had was a gift from God rather than a personal trophy generated from his own might, Nebuchadnezzar once again received his kingly authority and position. While in God's waiting room, the king learned that God is able to exalt the humble and to humble the self-exalted.

GOD CRAFTED COURAGE IN PETER

Young Peter was self-confident, almost to the point of cockiness. He spoke before he thought, made promises he could not keep, and made unwise decisions. He showed little concern for others, but wanted to make certain that his own investment in the Kingdom was going to pay rich dividends. As he passed through God's smelting process, Peter emerged refined as pure gold. He became a man of great courage as he stood before those who crucified the Lord and warned them to repent of their sins (Acts 2:22-23).

Peter's earlier courage came from self-reliance. But when he faced a life-threatening situation, he discovered that mere self-reliance was as firm as quicksand. His new courage came from a Holy Spirit reliance. When he acknowledged his own weaknesses and God's unlimited strength, Peter became confident in the power of the Lord. Like a small child who feels strong as long as he is with his big brother or his father, so did Peter feel quite adequate to carry out the Lord's commission because he knew that the Lord was with him.

GOD CRAFTED ABANDONMENT
TO HIS WILL IN PAUL

Then there was Saul, who did everything in his power to imprison and even put to death those who claimed to have a personal relationship with Jesus Christ. He was arrogant, zealous for the law and his religious traditions. He was convinced that his cause of persecuting Christians pleased God. After the Lord appeared to Saul on the road to Damascus, a spiritual revolution erupted in his life. He met the Lord and soon after became a devout follower of the One he had formerly persecuted. God began a good work in this young man and carefully crafted him into a magnificent missionary statesman, church planter, defender of the faith, and zealot for the cause of Jesus Christ. In fact, this man's life was so wrapped up in Christ that he later wrote to some friends, "To me, to live is Christ and to die is gain" (Philippians 1:21).

It takes time for a person to come to the place of complete surrender to God's will and direction because we have so many of our own ambitions to deal with. It's easy to sing, "All to Jesus I surrender, all to Him I freely give." But how often do we mean what we are singing? If we were honest with ourselves, we would have to sing, "Some to Jesus I surrender, some to Him I give with strings attached." If you were to list one area of life that you have found particularly difficult to abandon to God, what would it be? Your family? Ambitions? Friends? Failures? Money? Possessions? Future? Job?

Moses, Nebuchadnezzar, Peter, Paul, and others became totally different people as they experienced God's waiting room. They became better people, crafted people. But that's not the only benefit in waiting upon God.

WAITING ALLOWS GOD TO PREPARE YOU TO MINISTER TO OTHERS

One of my personal friends is Don Baker, who has served pastorates in Fresno, California; Portland, Oregon; and Rockford, Illinois. Our ministries overlapped when we both served churches in Fresno. In fact, we lived just one block from one another. I was aware that Don was experiencing some great hardship in his ministry due to some pressures in the church, but I did not know of a yet undiagnosed case of hypoglycemia. In his own words, Don expresses the pain he suffered as his whole world came crashing in on him:

> For years I had struggled to understand the unpredictable mood swings that could carry me from peaks of elation to the deep valleys of despair.
>
> I could preach with fervor and power, I could share Christ with enthusiasm and success. I would counsel with meaningful insight and socialize with sheer delight. But without warning, any or all of these positive and delightful emotions would suddenly be forced to give way to feelings of gloom and periods of weakness. I would withdraw, and a form of paranoia would settle in. I would suddenly be overwhelmed with feelings of inadequacy and inferiority. On occasion I toyed with thoughts of self-

destruction. . . .

The struggle reached its inevitable climax when I found myself too weak to minister, too filled with hostility to love, and too frightened to preach. One Sunday morning, I collapsed in tears. A dear brother in Christ, one of my deacons, found me convulsed with sobs, unable to rise and unwilling to even try.

In the weeks and months that followed, the bewildering and overpowering bouts with depression finally led me and my family to agree that the only direction left for me was to seek competent psychiatric care.

As I walked through the steel door into Ward 7E, my one thought was that the life I had known was finished. I would never again be able to enjoy the confidence of a congregation who would trust me to shepherd them.[1]

Why would God allow such devastating events to plague one of His choice servants? I don't claim to have the complete answer, but through these experiences, God was crafting Don for a special ministry to the hurting, both layman and clergy. The Lord has directed Don to write a series of books dealing with hard issues that few people even want to admit exist, such as discipline, forgiveness, depression, and other pertinent subjects, most of which came out of his own personal hurts and struggles.

The Scriptures support the fact that preparation for ministry is one of the reasons why God allows difficulties in life. Paul states, "Praise be to the God and Father of our Lord Jesus Christ, the Father of compassion and the God of all comfort, who comforts us in all our troubles, so that we can comfort those in any trouble with the comfort we ourselves have received from God. For just as the sufferings of

Christ flow over into our lives, so also through Christ our comfort overflows" (2 Corinthians 1:3-5).

It has often been said that music is a universal language. I believe that another universal language is suffering. As we go through our own problems and experience God's comfort, we have something to offer others who are experiencing great difficulties. People are not impressed with how much of the Bible we know, but they are impressed with how much we care. As we hurt and are comforted by God, we will learn to care for and comfort others as never before.

One of the greatest sources of comfort is the Psalms. But did you realize that many a psalm was hammered out on the anvil of conflict, as the psalmist reflected on his deep-water experiences? David testified of God's sustaining power as he penned, "But you are a shield around me, O LORD; you bestow glory on me and lift up my head. To the LORD I cry aloud, and he answers me from his holy hill. I lie down and sleep; I wake again, because the LORD sustains me" (Psalm 3:3-5).

These thoughts and emotions surfaced from within David's heart when he was in hiding from his son Absalom, who had stolen the hearts of the people and dethroned his father. Can you imagine the pain rushing through David's broken heart as he reflected on his rebellious son, whom he loved so dearly? How would you respond if members of your own family would like to see you out of the way; or your friends wanted to see you removed from your position of authority; or your colleagues changed their loyalty to someone else? David placed his faith in the Lord and trusted Him for sustaining grace.

One of the reasons I feel God placed me in a waiting room was so that I could encourage others through writing this book, as well as speaking at conferences and in churches. God has especially laid on my heart a ministry to pastors. I'm becoming increasingly aware that in many parts of the country it's "open season" on pastors. In fact, when I moved to Orange, California, I asked our district superintendent, Wally Norling, if he would mind me tagging along with him when he visited the pastors in our district. I told him that I wanted to give one day each month to eventually visit every pastor in the southwestern district of the Evangelical Free Church to learn what struggles they might be going through and to act as a resource person whenever needed.

Because the Lord has taught me so much through my own struggles, I would abuse my stewardship if I did not share the comfort and encouragement the Lord gave me. But in order to accomplish this mission, I realized I would need to be vulnerable and transparent. I could no longer afford the luxury of focusing on the successes of ministry. Instead, I would have to introduce the conflicts, doubts, fears, and failures. That is a risky undertaking. But when that waiting room experience provides an opportunity to see God in a new and intimate light, you have something worthwhile and potentially life-changing to share.

WAITING ALLOWS US AN OPPORTUNITY TO LEARN ABOUT GOD

When David sought the Lord, he asked Him, "Show me your ways, O LORD, teach me your paths; guide me in your truth and teach me, for you are God my Savior, and my hope is in you all day long" (Psalm 25:4-5). David wanted to learn about the Lord, to know the One he was serving, and to relate to Him as a Person rather than an ambiguous "man upstairs" who periodically looks over the rim of a cloud to see how man is doing.

GOD FULFILLS HIS PREPLANNED PURPOSE

David learned that God fulfilled a preplanned purpose in his life. He wrote, "I cry out to God Most High, to God, who fulfills his purpose for me" (Psalm 57:2). There were times of great turmoil in David's mind and mixed emotions when he was being pursued unjustly. Though he had already been anointed king, David was far from occupying a throne and ruling over the people. He was living like an outlaw: running, hiding, isolated from those he loved. He was no longer able to function as he once could. His cot was in a cave rather than a palace. His diet consisted of whatever he could find. But through it all, David was aware that God did have a plan for his life and would eventually fulfill it. David would one day be king. He would live in a palace and reign over his people with justice and righteousness.

As I was writing this, our neighbors were in the process of re-landscaping their yard. I mean four months of dust flying around the neighborhood, unwanted noise, and an ugliness that I felt was certain to send the house values to an all-time low. At times, trucks have blocked the street as they unloaded cement, dirt, or other materials. I never thought the house looked that bad in the first place, so I couldn't understand why they would want to re-landscape. The workers first removed plants, then shrubs, and then trees. Next to go was the driveway. They drained the water from the swimming pool and stored some of their tools in the pool. The place was a mess.

But as time passed, the workers completed the excavation and began to replant and rebuild. They put a spa in the corner of the backyard, complete with a gazebo; re-decked the swimming pool, laid a walkway between the pool and the spa, planted new shrubs and trees in both the front and back yards, placed a new driveway in front of the house, and built a three-foot wall around the front with two beautiful lamps to greet all visitors. After the ordeal was completed, both my wife and I commented on how beautifully it turned out and how wise our neighbors were to come up with such a plan.

As I reflected on that neighborhood episode, I saw a comparison between what was taking place next door and what we experience in God's waiting room. God also is in the landscaping business, only He works on the inner landscape. As we look at our lives, we feel that we're okay. There is nothing drastically wrong with us—no great sin staring us in the face. But what we don't notice are some of the weeds that have taken over the landscape. We fail to recognize that tiny insects have already laid their eggs, which have hatched and are eating away at some of the most vulnerable areas of our lives.

God may have to remove a plant, a shrub, or even a beautiful tree from our inner lives. He may have to uproot what we would like to hold on to. We may complain that God is ruining our lives. He is taking everything from us that we love. We may cry, "No, don't take that plant. I've been nurturing it for a long time. It has become so much a part of my life." And He in response says, "I know you have been nurturing it. And you have failed to see what it is doing to you. All of your time has been devoted to that little plant lately. You don't really need it. Besides, I want to replace it with something more lasting and satisfying." You may be telling yourself, "The more I pray and trust, the worse my life becomes. It has lost its beauty. It no longer has purpose or meaning. Everything I ever wanted has been taken away." What you need to understand is that God may be in the process of answering your prayers by cleaning out the old so that He can plant the new.

You may be at the point in life where God is beginning

to replace what He has taken from you. If you are, realize that just as the removing takes time, so does the replacing. You may not know how the landscape will look after it is completed, but rest assured that you have a Master Landscape Designer who knows exactly what He is doing, because He is operating according to a preplanned purpose for your life.

GOD IS TRULY A REFUGE

The psalmist found refuge in friends and caves, in foreign kingdoms and strange lands. But his greatest sanctuary came from the Lord. He declared, "I will sing of your strength, in the morning I will sing of your love; for you are my fortress, my refuge in times of trouble" (Psalm 59:16). A refuge is a place to escape to, a place of safety or refreshment.

Many years ago I made a trip to Banff, in Alberta, Canada. I was there for just an afternoon, having just completed a full day of an oral exam for my ordination into the ministry in nearby Calgary. But those few hours provided one of the most exhilarating experiences I have ever encountered. Banff is located in the beautiful Canadian Rockies, with their majestic cliffs. As I drove into the Rockies, I passed through Banff and headed about twenty minutes up the road. I pulled to the side of the road and made my way down to a spot where I could look over the Banff Valley, covered in the exquisite beauty of green pines, with the Banff Hotel nestled in the middle, like a chalet in the Alps.

The sky was dark blue, the temperature a comfortable 70 degrees, and there was no other human within a mile. I felt a little like Peter on the Mount of Transfiguration. I wanted to say, "Lord, I'd like to build a cabin right here on this site. This would be an ideal place for me to spend the rest of my life. Just think of all the meditation I could do."

As I sat and gazed on the beauty of God's creation, my ears began to hear the singing of birds, the trickling of a nearby creek, and the rustling of a little squirrel as he carried his treasure of food to his house in the tree. I started to sense the special aromas from the trees and plants that can only be appreciated in such an outdoor setting. Soon all my senses were activated by my surroundings. The idea of a refuge took on a new meaning for me as Banff became a place to which I could escape and renew my spirit. Life is filled with so many distractions that it is difficult to focus on God. A waiting room provides that opportunity.

GOD IS A DELIVERER

The psalmist also discovered God as One who was able to rescue him from many troubles: "I waited patiently for the LORD; he turned to me and heard my cry. He lifted me out of the slimy pit, out of the mud and mire; he set my feet on a rock and gave me a firm place to stand. He put a new song in my mouth, a hymn of praise to our God. Many will see and fear and put their trust in the LORD" (Psalm 40:1-3).

It is not uncommon to feel like you're in a slimy pit or up to your neck in the mud and mire of slander, innuendoes, or self-seeking, ambitious individuals, who use people and love mere things. You may come to appreciate the Lord as a deliverer when He moves you from such a place or circumstance and sets your feet on a rock. No longer will your feet be planted in midair. When He rescues you, God places you on solid ground and puts a song in your heart and praise on your lips.

If you have been wronged, remember that God has His own way of balancing the books. Solomon amplified this concept by writing, "Do not say, 'I'll pay you back for this wrong!' Wait for the LORD, and he will deliver you" (Proverbs 20:22). And when He delivers, He does so at the perfect time.

GOD WORKS WITHIN HIS OWN TIME SCHEDULE

When we wait, we are actually waiting for the Lord's time schedule as He works out His plan and purpose both in people and in circumstances. Although I had seriously considered leaving my ministry in Minnesota several times throughout the year before I made my decision, I can see now why I chose to stay. God was not ready to release me. Not only did He need to accomplish some things in my life, but He also was in the process of changing the heart of another pastor.

When I was in a countdown, hoping against hope during the month of January, 1986, a pastor in Orange, California was also wrestling with the possibility of moving to another ministry after a successful ten-year ministry. And so during that month, Mike Fisher announced that he would be concluding his ministry in Orange by the end of the school year, though he did not know where the Lord would lead him next. Several weeks after my resignation, I heard from Orange. God had His timetable set. I just had to wait until He arranged everything so that a position would open soon after I had resigned.

As you wait upon the Lord, you may see several of God's qualities in a new way. His faithfulness will take on a new meaning when you look back on these times of difficulty and identify how often the Lord met your need. You will understand better God's sustaining power when you wonder how you were able to keep from caving in. God's wisdom will be much appreciated when you find yourself making some good decisions and knowing that such wisdom did not originate from your own mind.

Waiting is beneficial in that it allows God time to complete His work in you, preparing you to minister to others and offering you an opportunity to learn more about God in intimate and new ways. But it also gives you time to make wise decisions.

WAITING GIVES YOU TIME
TO MAKE WISE DECISIONS

Some people take great pride in being quick decision makers, but when you observe their track record, you discover that their decisions were not always very wise. Either they made the decision without all the facts or they decided in the heat of the moment, allowing their emotions to control their judgment. Time will allow you to seek wise counsel from God.

We must guard against presuming upon our own wisdom when we make important decisions. The danger arises when we have been successful in the past with our decisions and assume that God must be so pleased with our wisdom that He is pouring out one blessing with another. So rather than consult Him for our next decision, we just move ahead, assuming that whatever we decide must be right. I'm reminded of the nation of Israel, who was in such a hurry to be like the nations around her that she did not wait for His counsel: "They soon forgot what he had done and did not wait for his counsel. In the desert they gave in to their craving; in the wasteland they put God to the test. So he gave them what they asked for, but sent a wasting disease upon them" (Psalm 106:13-15).

Some of us have a hard time asking directions when we and everyone else in the car know we don't have the foggiest idea where we are. But rather than stop for directions, our ego keeps us riding up and down the freeways, highways, and back roads, trying to find out where in the world we are and then how to get to where we are going. I know the problem and I still won't ask directions. And I am also painfully aware that there have been those times in life when I've tried every logical means to deal with a problem and make the right decision, only to arrive at dead ends and detours because I've failed to seek counsel from the One who could give me clear directions. During my waiting room experience I learned to ask a lot of directions from the Lord.

One further benefit from waiting for God is that you will have the opportunity to develop some new relationships with people whom you had known only casually or perhaps not at all. Trials cause true friends to surface, and some peripheral acquaintances transform into your greatest support system. At the same time, those who you thought were your strong foundation may turn out to be a mere mirage and crumble before your eyes. In pastoral circles it has been said that "the one who greets the pastor at the airport and helps him carry his bags is often the first one to encourage him to pack his bags and leave." I believe the same principle carries into many other relationships.

A pastor friend wrote to me after he had resigned under some duress. In his letter he expressed surprise that some of those he had thought were his intimate friends became distant, while others he knew only casually emerged into a strong support system for him and his family.

Linda and I were overwhelmed with the response of over six hundred letters after my resignation, from close friends as well as from individuals we hardly knew. They supported and encouraged us beyond our wildest expectations. Out of our experience, we have developed lifetime friendships. And today Minneapolis is a city we love to visit, not only for its beautiful lakes, trees, and clean air, but primarily because it is the home of so many dear and intimate friends.

Waiting on the Lord is never really easy, but when you take the time to wait in dependence on Him, it is worth all the trouble. The Scriptures promise, "The LORD longs to be gracious to you; he rises to show you compassion. For the LORD is a God of justice. Blessed are all who wait for him!" (Isaiah 30:18).

Indeed, God works in mysterious ways. They are foreign to us. Sometimes the Lord seems to be going against all logic. At other times everything makes perfectly good sense. I've learned I cannot put God in a box. He seldom operates the same way, even under identical circumstances. So I've had to allow God to be God.

My own testimony to God's faithfulness is expressed best in the words of the psalmist:

> Praise our God, O peoples, let the sound of his praise be heard; he has preserved our lives and kept our feet from slipping. For you, O God, tested us; you refined us like silver. You brought us into prison and laid burdens on our backs. You let men ride over our heads; we went through fire and water, but you brought us to a place of abundance. I will come to your temple with burnt offerings and fulfill my vows to you—vows my lips promised and my mouth spoke when I was in trouble. (Psalm 66:8-14)

I don't know how long you've been waiting on the Lord to do something in your life or in the circumstances that surround you. But realize that one of these days you will be leaving that waiting room.

NOTE: 1. Don Baker & Emery Nester, *Depression: Finding Hope and Meaning in Life's Darkest Shadow* (Portland: Multnomah Press, 1983), pages 15-16.

12

Leaving God's Waiting Room

The time was June 1955. I thought it would never arrive. For twelve years I had waited for this day and now it had come to pass: graduation from high school. Those dreary days of examinations, visits to the principal's office, and worries about grades were now behind me. It was time to celebrate, have a party, spend time with my friends, and talk about the good old days. And what about the future? It was too soon to be thinking about that. After all, I had at least three months before I'd be back in the same old routine of book reports, exams, and a new series of friends, which would be repeated two more times in graduate school (four years in seminary for a master's degree) and post graduate work (two more years for a doctorate).

One graduation was just preparing me to enter another period of study and another graduation, which was preparing me to repeat the cycle. That is something of what it is like leaving God's waiting room. You don't really leave it forever. Instead, your waiting room experience equips you to encourage others who are struggling and prepares you for future waiting room experiences.

Leaving God's waiting room is not the end of testing, nor is it a time to get careless. Instead, it is an occasion to savor everything that the Lord has revealed to you and make it a part of your life so that you will be better geared to face your future.

I discovered an interesting parallel in Jesus' temptation experience. Dr. Luke recorded the event as he wrote, "Jesus, full of the Holy Spirit, returned from the Jordan and was led by the Spirit in the desert, where for forty days he was tempted by the devil" (Luke 4:1). The Holy Spirit led Jesus to the place of temptation or testing, though He did not tempt the Lord. At that point, the Devil tempted Jesus with three powerful enticements. But Jesus defeated Satan at his game by using the Scriptures and by allowing the Holy Spirit to empower Him. Luke concludes the historical event with these words: "Jesus returned to Galilee in the power of the Spirit, and news about him spread through the whole countryside" (Luke 4:14).

The three implications that surfaced from this passage were (1) Jesus was led by the Spirit to His place of testing; (2) Jesus was sustained by the Spirit during the testing; and (3) Jesus left His place of testing in the power of the Spirit, now prepared to begin a three-year ministry that would change the course of human history. Each of these implications should be indicative of the believer in God's waiting room. The Holy Spirit leads him into the room, is available to sustain him during the testing, and will eventually lead him out and empower him in a new way for service, after leaving the waiting room.

As you leave this room, you will face two options. You can walk away from the testing with negative feelings, attitudes, and actions or you can choose to respond to your experience in a positive manner. Consider first how *not* to leave God's waiting room.

HOW NOT TO LEAVE GOD'S WAITING ROOM

Don't live in the past. Our memories often play tricks on us. Unless we have kept a detailed journal of our daily activities, we may forget what happened in the past. This causes us to go to one extreme or the other.

Some people remember only the bad events of the past. Therefore, everything seems negative when they reflect on what happened to them while they were waiting. Like the student who can only recall the exams, the low grades, or the times of embarrassment when called on to give a report, they recall nothing good—or the patient who can remember only the pain when he sits in the dentist's chair.

I wouldn't doubt that Moses was living with past negative memories when God called him to go down to Egypt and deliver Israel. Recall that Moses was wanted for murder in the land of Egypt. Though forty years had passed, Moses was painfully aware that many of his peers, who had been jealous of his former position and privileges, would have liked nothing better than to remind the present Pharaoh of Moses' crime, which had never been brought to trial. In spite of the good times, Moses could recall only the last few agonizing days of his life in Egypt. Therefore, he was in no hurry to respond to the Lord's call. He rehearsed before God all of the reasons why he was unqualified for the task, and finally pleaded, "O Lord, please send someone else to do it" (Exodus 4:13).

Then there are those, like my wife, who recall only the good events of the past. They forget the difficulties, the failures, the setbacks, and the negative people. I must admit when I reflect on my early days in Pennsylvania, my mind is flooded with good memories because most of my first twenty-three years of life were very positive. I knew everyone in our neighborhood by name. I was in every house on both sides of our street. It was customary to keep our doors unlocked, and with a mere knock, open a neighbor's door and enter their house. Other memories include the pre-television days known as "the golden era of radio." As I listened faithfully each night to my favorite programs, my imagination took me into a world of experience I could never have known any other way.

But I also remember those hot sticky nights when I tried to sleep without air conditioning; the fact that my dad had to travel between Lancaster and Pittsburgh for seven years, thus making my times with him limited to weekends; the fact that our means of transportation was limited primarily to either walking or the bus, since we didn't get our first car until I was thirteen years old; my difficulties in school during my high school days because I had no interest in studying; and the death of both my grandfathers. Perhaps between the two options—remembering only the bad times or remembering only the good—the latter is preferred, but still it distorts reality.

Why is it so wrong to live in the past? Those who remember only the negative aspects may become overly cautious and fail to move ahead with the Lord into God's next chapter for them. And those who can recall only the positive experiences may want so much to return to the past that they have difficulty moving into the future, especially if adversity awaits them.

This was Israel's problem. No sooner had the people experienced deliverance from Egyptian bondage than they ran into some difficulty. Moses captured their hostile attitude when he wrote, "In the desert the whole community grumbled against Moses and Aaron. The Israelites said to them, 'If only we had died by the LORD's hand in Egypt! There we sat around pots of meat and ate all the food we wanted, but you have brought us out into this desert to starve this entire assembly to death'" (Exodus 16:2-3).

On another occasion they were told that the land God had promised them was inhabited by giants. When the community heard that their future was going to be filled by one gigantic problem after another, they wanted out of the agreement:

> That night all the people of the community raised their voices and wept aloud. All the Israelites grumbled against Moses and Aaron, and the whole assembly said to them, "If only we had died in Egypt! Or in this desert! Why is the LORD bringing us to this land only to let us fall by the sword? Our wives and children will be taken as plunder. Wouldn't it be better for us to go back to Egypt?" And they said to each other, "We should choose a leader and go back to Egypt." (Numbers 14:1-4)

These people just weren't thinking straight. They had previously cried out to God for deliverance from their bondage. Now they wanted to return to their former lifestyle, which included the burden of slavery. This is not unlike the person who has been delivered by God's power from a difficult past, but later is enticed to return to his former life with all its problems.

Once you leave God's waiting room, there is no turning back. What has passed is past. The Lord does not expect you to live in that past. He wants you to move ahead, to trust Him for the next steps, and to seek His help when you face the giants of opposition. The Lord wants you to enjoy the new beginning He has established for you.

Don't think about what might have been, nor live with the regrets of not doing a better job. Don't become entrapped by the "if only" game: "If only I had not said what I did." "If only I had been a better father." "If only I had known then what I know now." Take to heart the words of the Lord through His prophet Isaiah when He said, "Forget the former things; do not dwell on the past. See, I am doing a new thing! Now it springs up; do you not perceive it? I am making a way in the desert and streams in the wasteland" (Isaiah 43:18-19).

Don't waste time justifying your decisions. While writing this, I came across a book entitled *Everything to Gain: Making the Most of the Rest of Your Life* by Jimmy and Rosalynn Carter. In it they describe the transition between the defeat for a second term in the White House and the new chapter of their lives. Former President Carter writes:

> Only later would we realize that many people have to accept the same shocking changes in their lives as we did that winter: the involuntary end of a career and an uncertain future; the realization that "retirement age" is approaching; the return to a home without the children we had raised there; new family relationships, for which there had been no preparation. And in our case, all this was exacerbated by the embarrassment about what was to us an incomprehensible political defeat and also by some serious financial problems that we had been reluctant to confront.[1]

He continues to describe how much more difficult this transition was for his wife, Rosalynn:

She went about her official duties with her chin up, but she found it impossible to accept the result of the election. Over and over she would raise the same questions: "How could the press have been so bad?" "Why didn't the people understand our goals and accomplishments?" "How could God have let this happen?"[2]

Then, in her own words, Mrs. Carter describes the decision she finally came to once she decided to write this book with her husband. She had wanted everyone to understand the whys and wherefores of each major decision her husband made in office because she felt the press had been so unfair. But she writes:

When I began working on my book, Edmund Morris, one of the country's leading presidential biographers, said to me, "Don't try to make your place in history. It's already made." Suddenly I realized that I didn't have to "set the record straight" in some combative way as I had originally intended. The events were all there for everyone to see. I didn't have to write them all down. I was free to write my story, the story of my life, and so my book became an autobiography.[3]

This was a helpful piece of advice for me. As I was going through a painful experience in our Minnesota church, I kept a journal of each day's events for eighteen months. I thought that sometime I might write about those days when I was a little more detached from the middle of the frenzy. I decided to undertake the assignment a few months after my resignation. To my amazement, I couldn't believe how easily the thoughts flowed. Within a few weeks,

I had the makings of a manuscript that I felt would be of significant help to anyone who was going through a period of struggle in his life.

However, before I sent the manuscript to the publisher, I decided I had better allow some friends to read it and provide some feedback. That proved to be an excellent decision because each person who read the manuscript agreed it would be a very helpful book for hurting people. But they also agreed that throughout the manuscript I was attempting to justify all my actions, giving evidence why I was right and "they" were wrong. It became a "me" and "them" routine.

When I first received the constructive criticism, I thought, "Wait a minute. Whose side are they on anyway?" But later reflection showed me that they were right. I didn't have to set the record straight. God alone is the Vindicator. He exonerates and He disciplines. I realized that I needed to commit those decisions to Him and invest my time in more constructive ways. This action would also help eliminate any feelings of bitterness.

If you have been in a lawsuit, experienced a financial reversal, gone through a divorce, or been released from a job, you have spent agonizing hours pondering over the whys and wherefores of your ordeal. You have tried to explain to friends and acquaintances how or why it happened. You want to set the record straight, but you discover that the more you explain, the more complicated and illogical it sounds. Accept this word of advice and stop trying to fit every decision or action into a tight little compartment. Your close friends know you well enough, and those who have suspicions about you probably will not accept your explanation anyway. Place the matter in the Lord's hands and let Him take care of the rest.

Don't be embittered against those who contributed to your

problems. The apostle Paul encouraged his readers, "Get rid of all bitterness, rage and anger, brawling and slander, along with every form of malice. Be kind and compassionate to one another, forgiving each other, just as in Christ God forgave you" (Ephesians 4:31-32).

A bitter attitude toward someone usually hurts the embittered person more than the one toward whom it is aimed. I've known individuals who have lived for years with inner emotional turmoil whenever they were around someone they despised. Though they exhibited a smile on the outside, they seethed with anger internally.

Wisdom needs to replace those feelings of anger and hurt. Solomon said it well when he wrote, "A man's wisdom gives him patience; it is to his glory to overlook an offense" (Proverbs 19:11). How does wisdom give a person patience? By helping the individual recognize that God is very much aware of his situation. An offender may seem to have gotten away with it, but the Lord has the final say in the matter.

One word of caution: When God does deal with the offender, don't gloat over the discipline like a child who enjoys watching his parents discipline his brother. The Scriptures warn, "Do not gloat when your enemy falls; when he stumbles, do not let your heart rejoice, or the LORD will see and disapprove and turn his wrath away from him" (Proverbs 24:17-18).

Bitterness does not motivate an offender to repent, apologize, or acknowledge that he has done anything wrong. The offender may go to his grave believing he was in the right. So what can you do about that? You're right: nothing. So why be bitter? Instead, turn that bitterness over to the Lord and get on with your life. Your offender is responsible to God and will not get away with anything at all that he has done to hurt you. But if you don't deal with the bitterness and hurt, you will probably fall into the trap of carrying those feelings and attitudes into God's next phase for your life.

Now that you know what not to do when you are leaving God's waiting room, consider several positive concepts that will help you to effectively enter the next major stage of your life.

HOW TO LEAVE GOD'S WAITING ROOM

Visualize the scene: Moses is an old man of about one hundred and twenty years. The entire first generation of Israelites is dead. And now this elderly statesman stands before the new generation that is preparing to enter the land of promise. His voice still strong, Moses thunders to the crowd of pioneers:

> When you have eaten and are satisfied, praise the LORD your God for the good land he has given you. Be careful that you do not forget the LORD your God, failing to observe his commands, his laws and his decrees that I am giving you this day. Otherwise, when you eat and are satisfied . . . then your heart will become proud and you will forget the LORD your God, who brought you out of Egypt, out of the land of slavery. (Deuteronomy 8:10-12,14)

If the people expected to enjoy their new freedom and to sustain the success God was about to give, they would have to remember the Lord—exactly what you and I must implement when we leave the waiting room. The idea of remembering conveys more than a mental recall of God's work in your life. Let me explain by highlighting four observations from this passage and one from a second passage.

REMEMBER THE LORD

"When you have eaten and are satisfied, *praise the LORD* your God for the good land he has given you" (Deuteronomy 8:10). Perhaps one of the greatest contributions my waiting room experience provided was the desire to praise the Lord in both private and public worship. In the past, I had thanked the Lord for His blessings but spent little time in praise. Whereas thanksgiving conveys an appreciation for something God has done for me, praise attributes honor and worthiness to God for who He is, whether I receive any benefit or not. How much more should I praise Him when He acts on my behalf by sustaining me during the tough times and leading me into a bright future. An ancient song encouraged praise from believers with these words: "It is good to praise the LORD and make music to your name, O Most High, to proclaim your love in the morning and your faithfulness at night" (Psalm 92:1-2).

The lawgiver Moses expressed a second way that his listeners could remember God: "Be careful that you do not forget the LORD your God, failing to *observe* his commands, his laws and his decrees that I am giving you this day" (Deuteronomy 8:11). Someone has said, "It's not what I don't understand about the will of God that bothers me, but it's what I do understand, but fail to apply." Remember the Lord by obeying what you already know He wants you to be and to do.

Moses continued, "He gave you manna to eat in the desert, something your fathers had never known, *to humble and to test you so that in the end it might go well with you*" (Deuteronomy 8:16). The method of remembering highlighted here is one of acknowledging that God has a purpose in the waiting room experience. For Israel the immediate purpose was one of humility and testing.

The Lord may have a different immediate purpose for you, but the ultimate purpose is "that in the end it might go well with you." You are not going through your difficulty by chance. The Lord is working out His purpose in your life, giving you a hope for your future.

Here is one more observation that I want to make from another passage of Scripture:

> Praise our God, O peoples, let the sound of his praise be heard; he has preserved our lives and kept our feet from slipping. For you, O God, tested us; you refined us like silver. You brought us into prison and laid burdens on our backs. You let men ride over our heads; we went through fire and water, but you brought us to a place of abundance. I will come to your temple with burnt offerings and *fulfill my vows to you*—vows my lips promised and my mouth spoke when I was in trouble. (Psalm 66:8-14)

What promises did you make to the Lord when you asked Him for help? What did you tell Him you would do or be if He delivered you from your troubles? That you would be a better parent? A better mate? More disciplined in your spiritual life? More committed to His will for your life? More responsible with your finances? More people-focused? More patient? Kind? Helpful? Understanding? Forgiving? Now is the time to begin carrying out what you have promised. Remember the Lord as you move on to the responsibility of building your new life.

BUILD A NEW LIFE

For some people, life does not change radically after they leave the waiting room, while others experience a significant difference. You may have begun a new life without your mate, child, parent, or friend. Life is just not what it used to be. Perhaps your new life includes a new job, a new location, or a new relationship.

One person may have to build new physical strength after major surgery. Another will focus on developing a whole new set of values and priorities because of what was learned in the waiting room. Still another establishes a life that has been honed out of failure and embarrassment.

The vital element in this principle is "building," which is the opposite of "tearing down." It means progress and not status quo. It demands change. To think the past was better than the present or future is to limit what God can and wants to do in your life. The apostle Paul took this plan of action when he wrote, "Forgetting what is behind and straining toward what is ahead, I press on toward the goal to win the prize for which God has called me heavenward in Christ Jesus" (Philippians 3:13-14). From God's perspective, the best is yet to come, as long as you don't repeat the mistakes of the past.

DETERMINE NOT TO REPEAT PAST MISTAKES

One purpose of tests in school is to determine whether you have learned the material or not. God's testing has a similar purpose. Failure to pass the test means repeating it. Israel is a good example of a people who had to repeat a test because they failed to learn what God had been teaching them. The psalmist provides a synopsis of Israel's history, revealing their repetition of sin against God:

> They forgot what he had done, the wonders he had shown them. . . . They willfully put God to the test by demanding the food they craved. . . . For they did

not believe in God or trust in his deliverance. . . . In
spite of all this, they kept on sinning; in spite of his
wonders, they did not believe. . . . How often they
rebelled against him in the desert and grieved him
in the wasteland! . . . They did not remember his
power—the day . . . he displayed his miraculous
signs in Egypt. (Psalm 78:11,18,22,32,40,42-43)

Repeated sin results in repeated discipline. Mistakes of the
past may not be the result of willful sin. In fact, they may not
be a violation of God's character or will, but rather the result
of not knowing how to work with or understand people.
They could also have been ignorance of good timing.
Whatever blunders you've made in the past, determine to
learn from them so that you don't repeat the error, fail the
test, and have to repeat it again. On a more positive note,
evaluate what God has already done for you.

ASSESS YOUR BLESSINGS

The song "Count Your Blessings" is sound advice. As I
penned these words, I decided to reflect on God's blessings
from the summer of 1985 to December of 1986. I wanted to
identify a number of the blessings Linda and I had experienced. What were the highlights of those eighteen
months? The following events describe only a partial list of
what accented that period:

1. *A speaking ministry for my wife and me at a Christian
camp in California.* The Lord blessed that ministry more
than any I had ever witnessed before. Those who attended
the meetings confirmed God's blessing by their own life
changes. (July 1985)

2. *The privilege of traveling to the Philippines and Hong
Kong to encourage pastors and missionaries.* That experience

made an indelible impression upon my mind and heart. I would never again be the same. God broke my heart with the realities of both physical and spiritual poverty, along with man's inhumanity to man. (October-November 1985)

3. *An opportunity to minister in Winnipeg, Canada, where I spoke about ministerial stress and burnout.* The pastors responded with great appreciation because many were experiencing an enormous amount of stress, and some had already entered the burnout phase. This prepared me for my own battle with stress when I returned to Minneapolis. As I got off the plane, I was informed that Linda had been in an accident and was in the hospital. Thus began my waiting room ordeal. (January 1986)

4. *The privilege to speak in my former church in Fresno, California.* This experience provided the much needed affirmation of God's hand upon my preaching ministry. During the transition, I had questioned whether I had lost that ability somewhere in the process. The positive response came at a time when it was most needed and appreciated. (September 1986)

5. *The Lord's provision of a new ministry according to the desires of my heart.* The people, location, and the freedom to be who God had made me to be all contributed to my conviction that God can be trusted with anything I am willing to place into His hands. (September 1986)

6. *An opportunity to give a week of messages at the seminary our son was attending, and to spend time with him.* Not only was the time with our son enjoyable, but the Lord anointed the ministry, encouraging both students and faculty alike. This ministry occurred when I was in God's waiting room and in transition between Minnesota and California. (October 1986)

7. *An extended period of time with our parents, both in Pennsylvania and Connecticut.* This was one of the most

refreshing times Linda and I have ever had. The Lord renewed my body and spirit. This time of refreshment transpired during our transition period when we needed a sense of stability. We felt the necessity to be near our "roots." (October-November 1986)

8. *The development of a strong support system of friends who sustained and encouraged us through the difficult times.* The friendships began as people ministered to us. But as time passed and the Lord strengthened us, we were able to minister to them. A permanent bonding of spirit and love resulted. (June 1986-December 1986)

Why not come up with your own list of God's blessings by putting down this book and identifying the highlights of the past twelve months. I'll prime the pump by asking a number of questions. Just take a separate sheet of paper and list those events or people who have given this past year a special meaning for you.

- How has God blessed you financially this year?
- How has He blessed you in your relationships with family, friends, or working companions?
- How has the Lord met your physical needs this year?
- What has God done in your own personal life in your character development? Attitude changes? Spiritual insights?
- In what ways are you different today than you were twelve months ago?
- What new positions, responsibilities, or job do you have today?
- List the names of some new friends you've developed over the past year.
- What positive changes have you seen in family members?

● What can you do today that you could not do a year ago?

● What skills have been developed during the year?

● Has there been a geographical move during the year? If so, describe the benefits of that move.

● What do you know today in a positive way that you did not know before?

● In what ways are you better equipped to face the unknowns of the future?

● With what truths about God have you become reacquainted? What new insights have you discovered about the Lord?

● What negative attitudes, circumstances, or issues has God removed from your life?

After you answer a number of these questions, you will have difficulty *not* praising the Lord. When David reflected on everything God had done for him, he responded:

"Who am I, O LORD God, and what is my family, that you have brought me this far? And as if this were not enough in your sight, O God, you have spoken about the future of the house of your servant. You have looked on me as though I were the most exalted of men, O LORD God.

"What more can David say to you for honoring your servant? For you know your servant, O LORD. For the sake of your servant and according to your will, you have done this great thing and made known all these great promises.

"There is no one like you, O LORD, and there is no God but you, as we have heard with our own ears. And who is like your people Israel—the one nation on earth whose God went out to redeem a people for himself, and to make a name for yourself, and to perform great and awesome wonders by driving out nations from before your people, whom you redeemed from Egypt? You made your people Israel your very own forever, and you, O LORD, have become their God." (1 Chronicles 17:16-22)

Sometimes we become blinded to everything the Lord has done for us because we busy ourselves in the battles of the day. We would do well to spend more time reflecting on what God has already done for us and less time bemoaning our present difficulties. Why not invest the next few moments to praise God from whom all blessings flow? As you commit yourself to a positive mind-set because of what God has already done, you will be taking the first step toward supporting others in God's waiting room. Now before you put away your pen and paper, consider recording one further list. What have you learned from your waiting room experience?

ASSESS YOUR LESSONS

As I reflected on my special time with God I jotted down some insights that have become very meaningful to me. For instance, I learned:

1. *God can be trusted.* "Great Is Thy Faithfulness." Perhaps this truth has penetrated my life more than any other fact about God. My experience affirms the psalmist's testimony: "For the word of the LORD is right and true; he is faithful in all he does" (Psalm 33:4).

2. *God does not make mistakes.* When I was in the midst of upheaval, I did question this proposition, but as I look back on the events of the past, I have complete confidence in the validity of this statement.

3. *God will vindicate and affirm those who seek Him.* To avoid trying to "set the record straight," I will not go into specifics at this point. I only want to state that the Lord has affirmed my decision to resign through many people and circumstances.

4. *Prayer works.* Specific prayer results in specific answers. Linda and I prayed for a specific type of ministry, a specific kind of house, and many specific affirmations of God's leading.

5. *God can still do the impossible.* For me, finding a new ministry after my own heart and a house that both Linda and I would agree on confirmed this truth.

6. *When I seek God for the process, He blesses the product.* I always prayed about issues, plans, and even sermons. But more often than not, my prayers were primarily for the Lord to bless what I had already decided I was going to do. Today, I seek Him in the process, for I am convinced that when He is invited into the process, He will prosper the product.

7. *There will be no real progress until you unconditionally surrender it all to God.* If you are willing to lose it all, you will gain more than you could possibly lose. I have no doubts that I have gained far more than I have lost. But I had to come to that place of unconditional surrender. No deals. No holding out. No holding on to something I wanted for myself. It all had to be given over to God. Contrary to the popular song, my theme is going to be "I did it His way."

8. *There is no security except in the Lord.* Neither money, job, friends, personal ability, nor past success can offer security. It can all be removed quickly. Only the stability of God is constant. I saw my job and my financial security removed. My past success and personal abilities were of little value. So I concluded that security could be found in God alone, and I was not disappointed.

9. *God will provide what I need and what is best for me*

(Isaiah 48:17). Today I have no doubt that I am experiencing His best. There were times when I told myself, "I don't need that." But now I reflect, "Yes, that's exactly what I needed, even though I didn't like it." At other moments I thought, "That opportunity would certainly be best for me," but today I tell the Lord, "Thank You for not taking me in that direction."

10. *I am responsible for being faithful to the Lord. He is responsible for my success.* At first, this may seem like an excuse for failure. But hear me out. If I focus on being successful, I may be tempted to compromise biblical principles in order to fulfill personal ambition. Therefore, I will strive for faithfulness to Him and let God decide the degree of success He wants me to experience. I will accept any failure that comes my way and not blame God that things didn't turn out the way I had hoped. I will also recognize that any measure of success will not be limited to my hard work, but rather will result from a combination of my faithfulness to the Lord and His desire to bless the work of my hands.

11. *I must not attempt to be what God has not designed me to be.* There will always be pressure from others who would like to make me in their own or someone else's image. I must keep myself under the control of the Holy Spirit and allow Him to affirm me to others. I am not God's gift to all people, but I am His gift to some, just as you are. Therefore, I must discern how He has gifted me and where and how He wants me to use those gifts.

12. *The most effective parenting skills I have developed are praying, listening, and advising when asked.* This has replaced my tendency to speak more and listen less. The relationship my wife and I have with our married children and daughters-in-law has become one of God's richest blessings.

13. *People want to be fed spiritually with bite-sized doses—* something they can chew over and digest throughout the

week. They are more interested in how God's truth has affected my life than about the facts of the Bible. They want to see Christianity lived out in someone's life, both in the struggles and the victories. If they can see the Lord at work in my life, then they are more willing to allow Him the same opportunity in their own lives.

How about your own lessons? What have you learned about God? Yourself? Relationships? Finances? The Scriptures? Your job? Faith? Trust? Why not take some time to identify those very important lessons the Lord has taught you in His waiting room. As these lessons become firmly implanted in your mind, you will have something to share with those who are still waiting.

BE A SUPPORT TO THOSE WHO ARE STILL WAITING

How amazed I was as I emerged from God's waiting room at how many others had either just entered or were in the midst of a waiting process. As people heard about my waiting experience, they became intensely interested in uncovering anything and everything I had learned.

Soon I concluded that the Lord was leading me to tell my story, which is really His story: an account of God's faithfulness and instruction to one who had so much to learn. So I've told my story in sermons, in counseling opportunities, and now in this book. And I pray that my transparency and vulnerability have become a light for your path and a hope for your future.

Several months into my waiting room experience, I began to sense that what I was experiencing would have a long-range effect both in my life and in the lives of others. One Sunday morning, I shared with my congregation that I was willing to be an object lesson for the Lord. If He wanted to break and reshape me in full view of my congregation,

He had my permission. If He wanted to show them how He could refine a person, He had my full cooperation. I've come to the conclusion that the Lord accepted my offer.

Likewise, your own waiting room experience is not valuable only to you. It can also profit others if you share the results with them.

The apostle Paul informed his readers why the Lord made certain that the events in the life of Israel would be recorded for the generations to follow:

> Now these things *occurred as examples*, to keep us from setting our hearts on evil things as they did. . . . These things *happened to them as examples* and were written down as warnings for us, on whom the ful-fillment of the ages has come. So, if you think you are standing firm, be careful that you don't fall! No temptation has seized you except what is common to man. And God is faithful; he will not let you be tempted beyond what you can bear. But when you are tempted, he will also provide a way out so that you can stand up under it. (1 Corinthians 10:6,11-13)

What has happened in your life needs to be shared in an appropriate manner at the proper time. You may find yourself talking to a friend or neighbor. Or perhaps you'll encourage a group of believers meeting in a Bible study or a Sunday school class. Whatever the forum and whenever the time, the fact is that you should share what you've learned with others who are still waiting. This will be a help to you and a great encouragement to others.

When the time comes for you to leave God's waiting room, remember the process Jesus went through when He was tempted by the Devil: (1) He was led by the Spirit into the wilderness; (2) He resisted the Devil in the power of the

Holy Spirit during His wilderness experience; (3) He was sustained by the Spirit throughout that experience; and (4) He left the wilderness in the power of the Holy Spirit.

I don't know where you are in regard to God's waiting room, but I do know that the Lord can be trusted. As you place your confidence in Him, you will be able to say with the psalmist, "He who dwells in the shelter of the Most High will rest in the shadow of the Almighty. I will say of the LORD, 'He is my refuge and my fortress, my God, in whom I trust.'. . . He will cover you with his feathers, and under his wings you will find refuge; his faithfulness will be your shield and rampart" (Psalm 91:1-2,4).

NOTE: 1. Jimmy and Rosalynn Carter, *Everything to Gain: Making the Most of the Rest of Your Life* (New York: Random House, 1987), page 4.
2. Carter, *Everything to Gain*, page 8.
3. Carter, *Everything to Gain*, page 16.

RICK YOHN

Rick Yohn is senior pastor of the Evangelical
Free Church of Orange, California. He served
previously as pastor at the Evangelical Free
Church of Fresno, California, and Grace
Church of Edina, Minnesota.

A native of Lancaster, Pennsylvania, Rick
graduated from Philadelphia College of the
Bible. He holds a Master degree in theology
from Dallas Theological Seminary and a
Doctor of Ministry degree from
Talbot Theological Seminary.

Rick is an effective communicator, both in his
preaching and his writing. He has a
commitment to helping people maximize their
potential. He speaks often at family and Bible
conferences, as well as college and seminary
campuses. His wife, Linda, is also a gifted
speaker and teacher. They have two sons,
Rick and Steven.

Rick Yohn is the author of several other
books, including his most recent book,
Living Securely in an Unstable World,
published by Multnomah Press.